THE STONE
THAT
ROLLED AWAY

AN ORIGINAL GUIDEPOSTS BOOK

The editors wish to express heartfelt thanks to
Book Designer and Illustrator Judy Pelikan for her sensitive art direction
and masterful touch in creating a book of visual beauty and originality.
Our sincere gratitude also goes to Production
Manager Sally Seamans and Production
Assistant Beverly Clausen for their gifted
collaboration with the designer in helping
her to realize her artistic vision throughout
The Stone That Rolled Away.

Printed in U.S.A.

THE STONE THAT ROLLED AWAY

Living the Miracle of Easter

Guideposts
Carmel, New York 10512

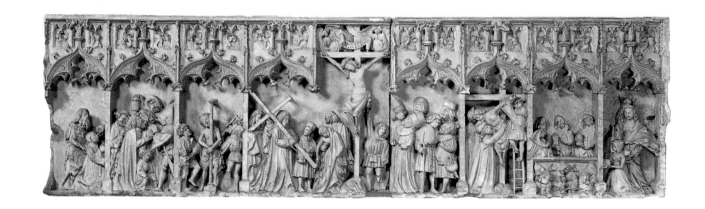

Table of Contents

1
The Easter Journey Begins

2
Praising The King

3

Cleansing the Temple

4

The Road to Calvary

5
Season of Miracles

6
The Farewell Feast

7
The Darkest Day

8

Rolling Stones Away

9

Letting Easter In

Introduction

ND very early in the morning on the first day of the week they went to the tomb when the sun had risen.

They had been saying to one another, "Who will roll away the stone for us from the entrance to the tomb?" But when they looked they saw that the stone — which was very big — had already been rolled back.

— *Mark 16:2-4 (NJB)*

Alleluia! He is Risen!

A triumphant ending…
a glorious morning…
a beautiful grace…
an enduring hope…
an everlasting joy…

ASTER. Its promises were born on a starry night in a little manger, grew to maturity on dusty roads and storm-tossed seas, died on a darkened hillside on a wooden cross between two thieves, and were miraculously fulfilled when a stone was rolled away and a tomb lay empty.

EASTER. The greatest hope that ever was. Without it, you and I lose faith, grow faint of heart, tremble in fear and doubt. Without Easter's miracle, why love? Why give? Why forgive? *Why live?* With Easter's triumphant Resurrection, we live each day with hope: We try, we fail, we go on. We start, we stop, we begin again. We reach out, we venture further, and we succeed. We seek, we ask, and we find. Because of Christ, we have new life. Because He lives, we live! And because He lives, *we can live the miracle of Easter every day.*

This is the promise that we invite you to celebrate in *The Stone That Rolled Away: Living the Miracle of Easter.* Each of the nine chapters centers on a momentous event during that holiest of weeks when Christ was crucified and raised from the dead. And throughout each chapter, you'll discover the hope and assurance that will help you live joyously today. Through stories, poems, hymns, prayers and meditations, you'll journey from Jesus' triumphant return to Jerusalem on Palm Sunday, through the Last Supper and the dark day of His Crucifixion, to His Resurrection. As you read *The Stone That Rolled Away*, it is our hope that you will experience the joy, the wonder and the blessings of the Easter message, and that your faith and love for God will be strengthened and renewed.

In Chapter 1, "The Easter Journey Begins," we prepare our hearts for the King. One way to prepare would be to read aloud "Easter: Road Map for Living" by Elizabeth Sherrill, a week-long family devotion, retelling the extraordinary events of Holy Week and its promise of new beginnings.

We welcome Christ into our lives in Chapter 2, "Praising the King," with poems and hymns, as well as stories from Sue Monk Kidd, Marjorie Holmes and others.

Chapter 3, "Cleansing the Temple," helps us to identify the barriers that keep us from God, and shows us how to get rid of them so that we can truly begin to worship Him in the temple of our hearts.

As you follow Jesus on "The Road to Calvary," Chapter 4, you will find words of hope and comfort in poetry, prayers and hymns from Isaac Watts to Annie Johnson Flint.

Then let Christ heal your pain and make you whole in Chapter 5, "Season of Miracles." Children also will delight in "Let the Children Come," Easter stories, poems and activities just for them.

In Chapter 6, "The Farewell Feast," you will learn the meaning of servant-hood and how to keep Jesus' command to love one another.

Then experience the events surrounding the Crucifixion in "The Darkest Day," Chapter 7, where you will learn to see the cross as God's way of bringing us through suffering to everlasting joy.

Celebrate Jesus' glorious Resurrection in Chapter 8, "Rolling Stones Away." There you will discover the possibilities of new beginnings with stories like Marilyn Morgan Helleberg's "The Impossible Stone" and "The Easter Sun Dance" by David Rochford.

And, finally, with thanksgiving for the promise fulfilled, we invite you to open your heart in Chapter 9 by "Letting Easter In." Not only will you be inspired to keep Easter alive every day, all year long, but you also will find sustenance from the favorite holiday recipes to try in "Easter Blessings From Our Table."

May blessings and joy overflow as you journey through this holy season in the pages of *The Stone That Rolled Away*. May you experience more and more of God's unconditional and everlasting love. And may all your days be filled with new beginnings of hope and praise because of that triumphant, bright morning when the stone was rolled away.

Alleluia! Alleluia!

– The Editors

The Greatest Week:
The Story of Easter

The Triumphant Entry into Jerusalem

S they approached Jerusalem, near the towns of Bethphage and Bethany, they came to the Mount of Olives. Jesus sent two of his disciples on ahead with these instructions: "Go to the village there ahead of you. As soon as you get there, you will find a colt tied up that has never been ridden. Untie it and bring it here. And if someone asks you why you are doing that, tell him that the Master needs it and will send it back at once."

So they went and found a colt out in the street...

They brought the colt to Jesus, threw their cloaks over the animal, and Jesus got on. Many people spread their cloaks on the road, while others cut branches in the field and spread them on the road. The people who were in front and those who followed behind began to shout, "Praise God! God bless him who comes in the name of the Lord! God bless the coming kingdom of King David, our father! Praise be to God!" ...

Jesus Goes to the Temple

The next day... when they arrived in Jerusalem, Jesus went to the Temple and began to drive out all those who were buying and selling. He overturned the tables of the money-changers and the stools of those who sold pigeons, and he would not let anyone carry anything through the Temple courtyards. He then taught the people: "It is written in the Scriptures that God said, 'My Temple will be called a house of prayer for the people of all nations.' But you have turned it into a hideout for thieves!"

The chief priests and the teachers of the Law heard of this, so they began looking for some way to kill Jesus. They were afraid of him, because the whole crowd was amazed at his teaching....

The Plot against Jesus

It was now two days before the Festival of Passover and Unleavened Bread. The chief priests and the teachers of the Law were looking for a way to arrest Jesus secretly and put him to death. "We must not do it during the festival," they said, "or the people might riot."

Judas Agrees to Betray Jesus

Then Judas Iscariot, one of the twelve disciples, went off to the chief priests in order to betray Jesus to them. They were pleased to hear what he had to say, and promised to give him money. So Judas started looking for a good chance to hand Jesus over to them.

Jesus Eats the Passover Meal with His Disciples

On the first day of the Festival of Unleavened Bread, the day the lambs for the Passover meal were killed...when it was evening, Jesus came [to the upstairs room] with the twelve disciples. While they were at the table eating, Jesus said, "I tell you that one of you will betray me—one who is eating with me."

The disciples were upset and began to ask him, one after the other, "Surely you don't mean me, do you?"

Jesus answered, "It will be one of you twelve, one who dips his bread in the dish with me. The Son of Man will die as the Scriptures say he will; but how terrible for that man who will betray the Son of Man! It would have been better for that man if he had never been born!"

The Lord's Supper

WHILE they were eating, Jesus took a piece of bread, gave a prayer of thanks, broke it, and gave it to his disciples. "Take it," he said, "this is my body."

Then he took a cup, gave thanks to God, and handed it to them; and they all drank from it. Jesus said, "This is my blood which is poured out for many, my blood which seals God's covenant. I tell you, I will never again drink this wine until the day I drink the new wine in the Kingdom of God."

Then they sang a hymn and went out to the Mount of Olives.

Jesus Predicts Peter's Denial

ESUS said to them, "All of you will run away and leave me, for the scripture says, 'God will kill the shepherd, and the sheep will all be scattered.' But after I am raised to life, I will go to Galilee ahead of you." Peter answered, "I will never leave you, even though all the rest do!"

Jesus said to Peter, "I tell you that before the rooster crows two times tonight, you will say three times that you do not know me."

Peter answered even more strongly, "I will never say that, even if I have to die with you!"

And all the other disciples said the same thing.

Jesus Prays in Gethsemane

They came to a place called Gethsemane, and Jesus said to his disciples, "Sit here while I pray." He took Peter, James, and John with him. Distress and anguish came over him, and he said to them, "The sorrow in my heart is so great that it almost crushes me. Stay here and keep watch."

He went a little farther on, threw himself on the ground, and prayed that, if possible, he might not have to go through that time of suffering. "Father," he prayed, "my Father! All things are possible for you. Take this cup of suffering away from me. Yet not what I want, but what you want."

Then he returned and found the three disciples asleep. He said to Peter, "Simon, are you asleep? Weren't you able to stay awake for even one hour?" And he said to them, "Keep watch, and pray that you will not fall into temptation. The spirit is willing, but the flesh is weak."

He went away once more and prayed, saying the same words. Then he came back to the disciples and found them asleep; they could not keep their eyes open. And they did not know what to say to him.

When he came back the third time, he said to them, "Are you still sleeping and resting? Enough! The hour has come! Look, the Son of Man is now being handed over to the power of sinful men. Get up, let us go.

Look, here is the man who is betraying me!"

The Arrest of Jesus

Jesus was still speaking when Judas, one of the twelve disciples, arrived. With him was a crowd armed with swords and clubs and sent by the chief priests, the teachers of the Law, and the elders. The traitor had given the crowd a signal: "The man I kiss is the one you want. Arrest him and take him away under guard."

As soon as Judas arrived, he went up to Jesus and said, "Teacher!" and kissed him. So they arrested Jesus and held him tight....

Then all the disciples left him and ran away....

Jesus before the Council

Then Jesus was taken to the High Priest's house, where all the chief priests, the elders, and the teachers of the Law were gathering. Peter followed from a distance and went into the courtyard of the High Priest's house. There he sat down with the guards, keeping himself warm by the fire. The chief priests and the whole Council tried to find some evidence against Jesus in order to put him to death, but they could not find any. Many witnesses told lies against Jesus, but their stories did not agree.

Then some men stood up and told this lie against Jesus: "We heard him say, 'I will tear down this Temple which men have made, and after three days I will build one that is not made by men.'" Not even they, however, could make their stories agree.

Peter Denies Jesus

Peter was still down in the courtyard when one of the High Priest's servant girls came by. When she saw Peter warming himself, she looked straight at him and said, "You, too, were with Jesus of Nazareth."

But he denied it. "I don't know... I don't understand what you are talking about," he answered, and went out into the passageway. Just then a rooster crowed.

The servant girl saw him there and began to repeat to the bystanders, "He is one of them!" But Peter denied it again.

A little while later the bystanders accused Peter again, "You can't deny that you are one of them, because you, too, are from Galilee."

Then Peter said, "I swear that I am telling the truth! May God punish me if I am not! I do not know the man you are talking about!"

Just then a rooster crowed a second time, and Peter remembered how Jesus had said to him, "Before the rooster crows two times, you will say three times that you do not know me." And he broke down and cried.

Jesus before Pilate

Early in the morning the chief priests met hurriedly with the elders, the teachers of the Law, and the whole Council, and made their plans. They put Jesus in chains, led him away, and handed him over to Pilate. Pilate questioned him, "Are you the king of the Jews?"

Jesus answered, "So you say."

The chief priests were accusing Jesus of many things, so Pilate questioned him again, "Aren't you going to answer? Listen to all their accusations!"

Again Jesus refused to say a word, and Pilate was amazed.

Jesus Is Sentenced to Death

T every Passover Festival Pilate was in the habit of setting free any one prisoner the people asked for. At that time a man named Barabbas was in prison with the rebels who had committed murder in the riot. When the crowd gathered and began to ask Pilate for the usual favor, he asked them, "Do you want me to set free for you the king of the Jews?" He knew very well that the chief priests had handed Jesus over to him because they were jealous.

But the chief priests stirred up the crowd to ask, instead, that Pilate set Barabbas free for them. Pilate spoke again to the crowd, "What, then, do you want me to do with the one you call the king of the Jews?"

They shouted back, "Crucify him!"

"But what crime has he committed?" Pilate asked.

They shouted all the louder, "Crucify him!"

Pilate wanted to please the crowd, so he set Barabbas free for them. Then he had Jesus whipped and handed him over to be crucified.

The Soldiers Make Fun of Jesus

The soldiers took Jesus inside to the courtyard of the governor's palace and called together the rest of the company.

They put a purple robe on Jesus, made a crown out of thorny branches, and put it on his head. Then they began to salute him: "Long live the King of the Jews!"

They beat him over the head with a stick, spat on him, fell on their knees, and bowed down to him. When they had finished making fun of him, they took off the purple robe and put his own clothes back on him. Then they led him out to crucify him.

Jesus Is Crucified

On the way they met a man named Simon, who was coming into the city from the country, and the soldiers forced him to carry Jesus' cross.

(Simon was from Cyrene and was the father of Alexander and Rufus.) They took Jesus to a place called Golgotha, which means "The Place of the Skull." There they tried to give him wine mixed with a drug called myrrh, but Jesus would not drink it. Then they crucified him and divided his clothes among themselves, throwing dice to see who would get which piece of clothing. It was nine o'clock in the morning when they crucified him. The notice of the accusation against him said: "The King of the Jews." They also crucified two bandits with Jesus, one on his right and the other on his left.

People passing by shook their heads and hurled insults at Jesus: "Aha! You were going to tear down the Temple and build it back up in three days! Now come down from the cross and save yourself!"

In the same way the chief priests and the teachers of the Law made fun of Jesus, saying to one another, "He saved others, but he cannot save himself! Let us see the Messiah, the king of Israel, come down from the cross now, and we will believe in him!"

And the two who were crucified with Jesus insulted him also.

The Death of Jesus

At noon the whole country was covered with darkness, which lasted for three hours. At three o'clock Jesus cried out with a loud shout, "*Eloi, Eloi, lema sabachthani?*" which means, "My God, my God, why did you abandon me?"

Some of the people there heard him and said, "Listen, he is calling for Elijah!"

One of them ran up with a sponge, soaked it in cheap wine, and put it on the end of a stick. Then he held it up to Jesus' lips and said, "Wait! Let us see if Elijah is coming to bring him down from the cross!"

With a loud cry Jesus died.

The curtain hanging in the Temple was torn in two, from top to bottom. The army officer who was standing there in front of the cross saw how Jesus had died. "This man was really the Son of God!" he said.

Some women were there, looking on from a distance. Among them were Mary Magdalene, Mary the mother of the younger James and of Joseph, and Salome. They had followed Jesus while he was in Galilee and had helped him. Many other women who had come to Jerusalem with him were there also.

The Burial of Jesus

It was toward evening when Joseph of Arimathea arrived. He was a respected member of the Council, who was waiting for the coming of the Kingdom of God. It was Preparation day (that is, the day before the Sabbath), so Joseph went boldly into the presence of Pilate and asked him for the body of Jesus....Pilate told Joseph he could have the body. Joseph brought a linen sheet, took the body down, wrapped it in the sheet, and placed it in a tomb which had been dug out of solid rock. Then he rolled a large stone across the entrance to the tomb. Mary Magdalene and Mary the mother of Joseph were watching and saw where the body of Jesus was placed.

The Resurrection

AFTER the Sabbath, as Sunday morning was dawning, Mary Magdalene and the other Mary went to look at the tomb. Suddenly there was a violent earthquake; an angel of the Lord came down from heaven, rolled the stone away, and sat on it. His appearance was like lightning, and his clothes were white as snow. The guards were so afraid that they trembled and became like dead men.

The angel spoke to the women. "You must not be afraid," he said. "I know you are looking for Jesus, who was crucified. He is not here; he has been raised, just as he said. Come here and see the place where he was lying. Go quickly now, and tell his disciples, 'He has been raised from death, and now he is going to Galilee ahead of you; there you will see him!' Remember what I have told you."

So they left the tomb in a hurry, afraid and yet filled with joy, and ran to tell his disciples.

Suddenly Jesus met them and said, "Peace be with you." They came up to him, took hold of his feet, and worshiped him. "Do not be afraid," Jesus said to them. "Go and tell my brothers to go to Galilee, and there they will see me."

...

Jesus Appears to His Disciples

The eleven disciples went to the hill in Galilee where Jesus had told them to go.

When they saw him, they worshiped him, even though some of them doubted.

Jesus drew near and said to them, "I have been given all authority in heaven and on earth. Go, then, to all peoples everywhere and make them my disciples: baptize them in the name of the Father, the Son, and the Holy Spirit, and teach them to obey everything I have commanded you. And I will be with you always, to the end of the age."

From the Good News Bible (TEV) • Mark 11:1-4, 7-10, 15-18 • Mark 14:1-2, 10-12, 17-46, 50, 53-59, 66-72 • Mark 15:1-43, 45-47 • Matthew 28:1-10, 16-20.

A Crimson-Bright Easter

WHAT does it mean to me personally —
the stone rolled away,
the empty tomb,
the angel's message:
He is not here; He is risen.

This, surely this —
that on the final page
of my brief life
it shall not read
in dull, dead black,
The End;
but crimson-bright,
indelible and shining there,
To Be Continued!

— *Helen J. Fricke*

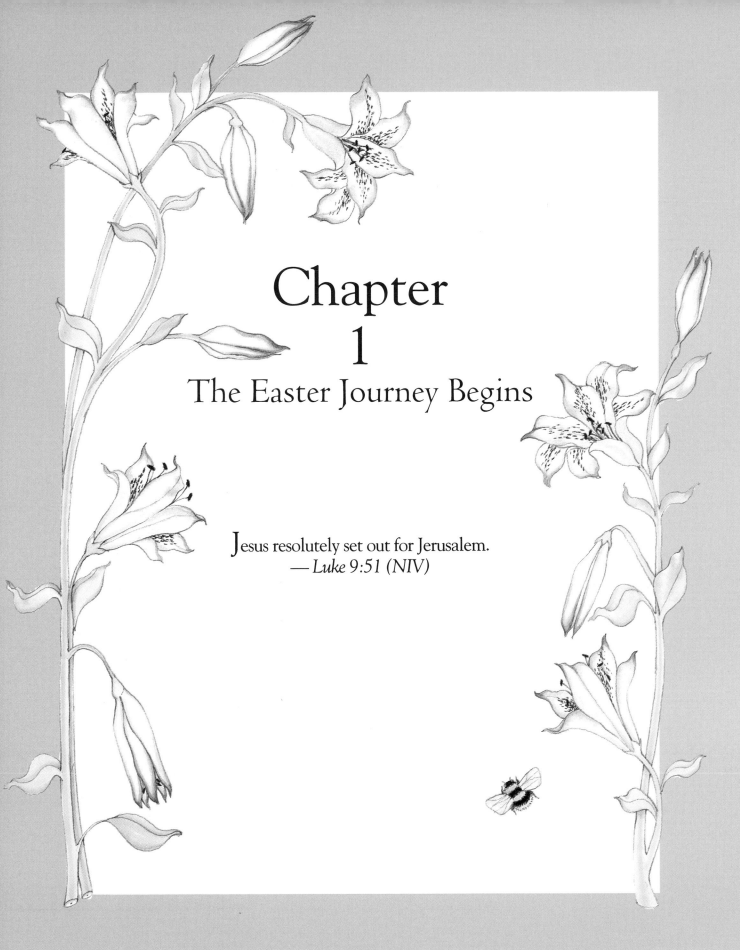

Chapter
1
The Easter Journey Begins

Jesus resolutely set out for Jerusalem.
— *Luke 9:51 (NIV)*

Easter: Road Map For Living

Elizabeth Sherrill

SATURDAY BEFORE PALM SUNDAY

The Easter Journey

And they were on the road, going up to Jerusalem....
— *Mark 10:32 (RSV)*

THEY were on a journey to Easter, these first followers of Jesus. They had only hints of their destination, but they followed gladly because they had come to trust the Man Who led the way.

You and I make this journey to Easter all our lives — following Him again and again from death into life. But we have an advantage those earliest disciples did not have — a road map of the way ahead.

Holy Week is the road map of our journey.

The days leading to that first Easter form a pattern, which remains the same today. Those who experienced the wonder of the Resurrection had first to follow Jesus along the bewildering path of the previous week...and so must we. Each day in Holy Week corresponds to a step in our own walk toward the promise of God: beyond every ending a new beginning.

Different people will be at different places on the way. Whether it's Palm Sunday in your life, ringing with Hosannas, or Good Friday, dark with grief, the end of the road is the same: the empty tomb where what was lost has been given back, new and more glorious than before.

Those who walked that final week with Jesus did not know the unquenchable joy awaiting them. We know. And so we make the journey over these next eight days with the Easter song already on our lips.

The Struggle Begins

And the crowds...shouted,"Hosanna to the Son of David!"
— Matthew 21:9 (RSV)

THE cheering throngs, the waving palm branches, brought still more people crowding to the side of the road. Those in front passed the news to those behind: "Yes, riding a donkey!" The loaded words spread swiftly. Five hundred years earlier, Zechariah had foretold the restoration of David's kingdom. The occupied nation had not forgotten this prophecy, nor the manner in which the son of David would enter Jerusalem: mounted on a donkey....

At last, at last, the King had come! Tomorrow they would be free from Rome's hated rule. Many tore the very clothes from their backs and spread them in the street for the animal to step on, to be snatched up again and worn with pride at the coming coronation, saying proudly: *I was there when He entered Jerusalem!*

Holy Week begins as every Christian walk begins, with Jesus coming into our lives. Our individual Palm Sunday may be as public as that first one: a religious rally, an eager crowd. For others, as it was for me, the event is quieter, more personal. But always a palm branch waves in our hearts: *He is here...at last, at last!*

And once He has made His triumphal entry into our hearts, we experience "little Palm Sundays" all along the way. Each time we receive love or forgiveness — and recognize that it is God Who is entering our lives in this way — we are once more standing on the royal road, welcoming the King. Palm Sunday represents all our personal encounters with God.

And only that. Some of the people who cried Hosanna on that first Palm Sunday mistook their personal experience for the whole of the truth. They had seen the Savior, they believed the battle was over. They mistook the beginning for the end. They thought the struggle was behind them; in fact the fiercest fight was just ahead.

MONDAY

The Cleansing

*And Jesus...drove out all who sold and bought
in the temple, and he overturned the tables of the money-changers
and the seats of those who sold pigeons.
— Matthew 21:12 (RSV)*

T was an unheard-of scandal! This young rabbi who yesterday had the whole city in a patriotic uproar today stormed into the very Temple precinct itself and created chaos. Doves flapping, men shouting, women scrabbling after the rolling coins. This fellow from Galilee, once again stirring up trouble!

But stirring-up is always what happens when Jesus enters the scene. Monday of Holy Week has its parallel in our individual journey of faith. He comes — and priorities are overturned, assumptions swept aside. The first thing He did on entering Jerusalem is the first thing He does on entering a life: He goes straight to the Temple — to the place where we worship — and cleans out whatever is not part of God's design. The process is called by many names: sanctification, amendment of life, getting right with God, but the meaning is the same. The recognition that with Jesus in charge, many things we used to do, say, want, are no longer okay. It's such a common pattern that we've come to expect it.

And there's the danger in the Monday experience. We think we know what things He wants to get rid of. When my mother was growing up, the list included wearing makeup, reading novels and riding a bicycle on Sunday. Each group, each era, has its own expectations.

But the hallmark of that Monday in Jerusalem was surprise. Jesus knew what stood between people in those days and God. "Astonished" is how Mark describes people's reactions to that original cleansing, and astonished is how we feel when God's housecleaning — not the one we envisaged — gets under way within us. Prejudice. Old hurts. A sense of inferiority. Whatever blocks our relationship with Him, out it must go.

"What are You doing?" we cry when the Cleanser strides in.

"I'm making Myself a temple," He replies.

Taking the Road to Calvary

And he was teaching daily in the temple.
— *Luke 19:47 (RSV)*

THERE was room in the Temple courtyard now. With the money tables gone, the baskets carted off, the great court was quiet, open. And into that vacated place the people poured to hear Him.

That's how it is in the Tuesdays of our lives. When His housecleaning clears away the clutter and He opens up space — in our schedules, in our hearts — then we hunger to fill that receptive space with knowledge of Him. This third day of Holy Week corresponds to the time in our lives when we drive two hundred miles to hear an inspired preacher, when we go without lunch to buy the latest teaching tape, or spend our week's vacation at a church retreat.

What teaching it was, there in the Temple! Jesus saw a widow drop a penny into the treasury, and taught about sacrificial giving. He was shown a coin with Tiberius' profile, and taught about priorities.

But Tuesday is not yet Easter Sunday. That is the risk on this part of our walk, that we'll be content with head knowledge and fail to complete the journey. All of us know people who stop at Tuesday. They attend three Bible studies, run from conference to conference — and never encounter the risen Lord.

Tuesday is a dangerous day for me. I love to study just for the sake of study. The sight of a fresh notebook makes my pulses speed. I can take beautifully outlined notes of a lecture without relating a word the speaker says to my own life. There must have been many like me who heard Jesus teach, that first Holy Week. There were crowds in the Temple, only a handful at the empty tomb.

But Jesus will not let us stop short of Easter, not forever. The time comes to close the books, to leave the lecture hall. To take the road to Calvary and beyond.

Touching the Supernatural

*And the blind and the lame came to him
in the temple, and he healed them.
— Matthew 21:14 (RSV)*

MIND and body. Reason and miracle. Jesus' ministry included both, this final week as always. In the clean-swept Temple He taught and He also healed. He asked men to understand, and He performed what surpasses understanding. As the blind saw and the lame walked, cries of wonder echoed along the marble porticoes, and the crowd swelled till Temple authorities took fresh alarm. Even more than brilliant teaching, miracles will always draw throngs. Wednesday's miracles of healing kept the city in a fever of excitement.

I've felt that excitement on the Wednesdays of my own life. I've seen it in the great arenas where today's charismatic healers draw their thousands. I've known the ecstatic gratitude when, for instance, my husband was instantaneously healed of cancer. This fourth day in Holy Week represents those times when our natural lives touch the supernatural. When here on earth we are caught up in the divine mystery.

But still we are not at the best. We stand wonderstruck but short of Easter. How strange it is, this journey we're embarked on. On Wednesday we seem to have arrived at the very throne room of God — and yet the road leads on, out into the dark.

How many of those who were healed there in the Temple followed Jesus to the end? "Though he had done so many signs before them," John writes of that last week, "yet they did not believe in him" (John 12:37, RSV). For Jesus, healing was always a sign, a pointer to something greater and better.

Better than health? Greater than an end to pain? Yes, He answers, follow Me and see! Unspeakable pain lay just ahead for Jesus, but He embraced it for the sake of that better thing. The road to Easter does not remain on the mountaintop of miracle. It leads down, through death to life everlasting.

The Power that Never Fails

Peter said to him, "Even if I must die with you, I will not deny you."
And so said all the disciples.
— Matthew 26:35 (RSV)

THE triumphal entry into Jerusalem. The cleansing of the Temple. The teaching and the miracles. All displayed their leader's power, and the faith of the disciples soared. Now, on this fifth day of the week, came the most intimate moment of all, the Passover meal, that high holy feast, just the twelve and Jesus. Over and over, at table, He reiterated His love for them, even kneeling before them to wash their travel-weary feet.

If they had ever doubted, they could no longer do so. What if, as Jesus cautioned, testings and trials lay just ahead. They could face anything. "Lord," Peter assured Him, "I am ready to go with you to prison and to death" (Luke 22:33, RSV).

Maundy Thursday corresponds to those times in our own lives when our faith feels unassailable. Surrounded by so many proofs of His love, how could we ever doubt?

Thursday is the most perilous day of our pilgrimage.

Because, when the test comes, we so often fail. Before daybreak Peter was swearing he'd never heard of Jesus. Maundy Thursday represents our failures, too — following swiftly on our moments of high commitment. The times when, having made great promises, we fall on our faces. When we let God down and let ourselves down and are left with only the certainty of our own weakness.

Yet strangely, Thursday also ushers in the most hopeful stage of our journey. Because at last we are truly on the road to Easter. We have learned better than to place our trust in ourselves. "I tell you, Peter," Jesus replied to Peter's confident boast, "the cock will not crow this day, until you three times deny that you know me" (Luke 22:34, RSV).

But He said it without condemnation, without rejection. Jesus knew that the way leads through loss. Loss of self-satisfaction and self-sufficiency. He knew that on the other side of Easter, Peter would find the power that never fails.

The Coming of Everlasting Joy

And they crucified him....
— Mark 15:24 (RSV)

I T was the darkest day. The unbearable day. Many who had followed Jesus up to now fled from the events of Friday. And those who stayed to watch wept in horror.

The rigged trial, the mob that howled for the blood of the Man Who had failed to meet their patriotic expectations. The brutal beating, the savagery of the soldiers, the stumbling walk through the city He had entered to cheers five days before. Finally, the nails pounded into flesh, the tortured body jerked upright, the naked Man dying by inches as His enemies jeered.

To have it end like this, after all the bright promise! It was not just the cruel death of the disciples' young leader, but the death of their faith, the end of all they believed in, on this black Friday that seemed anything but good.

Most of us have experienced this Friday for ourselves. It's not the disillusionment of Thursday, when our own performance falls short. It's the blow that strikes from outside, the tragedy that destroys our loved one, our health, our livelihood. We feel, as the disciples did on that terrible day, that Jesus Himself has failed us. If He were really God's Son, things like this could not happen. "Are you not the Christ? Save yourself and us!" (Luke 23:39, RSV).

There is no way around the Fridays of our lives, only the way through — through pain and death and burial. As His sorrowing followers laid Jesus in the tomb, so we lay down the wreckage of our hope. Ahead was Easter Sunday, but on Friday they couldn't know that. And neither can we, in the first shock of loss. We can only know that we will know. We can only know that the whole story is not yet told.

For, of course, Jesus is the Christ. He is saving us, whatever the appearance. He is bringing about our everlasting joy, in a way only God could have chosen. If it is Friday in your life today, Easter cannot be far away.

The Motions of Faith Sustain Us

On the sabbath they rested according to the commandment.
— Luke 23:56 (RSV)

FTER the din and tumult of that terrifying Friday came this day of absolute silence. It was the Sabbath, the day of rest. No clatter of hooves came from the deserted streets, no sing-song of water sellers.

Behind some of those shuttered doorways the silence was doubly deep. Here and there, in homes about the city, Jesus' former followers huddled in a stillness, not of reverence, but of the grave. For them all was finished. The future had been buried with their leader; they had nothing more to live for.

More than once in my own life I have wondered: Which is harder, the day of disaster or the day that follows? During an emergency we experience the rush of adrenalin, the numbness of shock. But what is there to sustain us in the empty aftermath, when our joy has died but we must go on living? Holy Saturday is that dark tunnel where we find ourselves when the light of faith goes out.

To keep us going when there is no point — that is the wisdom of religious tradition. What did Jesus' devastated followers do, on that silent Saturday? They kept the letter of the Law. They observed the Sabbath. There can't have been much conviction, for them, behind this weekly formality. They had only habit to get them through the hours.

But they did have habit. "Going through the motions" is usually condemned as meaningless for the walk of faith. Going to church when we no longer believe, reciting prayers we no longer mean. But when such things are all we can do, the motions of faith can keep us going...until the meaning comes.

The Joy that Invades Our Hearts

He is not here; for he has risen....
— Matthew 28:6 (RSV)

ONLY a week had passed since that triumphant Palm Sunday entrance into Jerusalem — but what a difference in the little procession that set out now! No cheering crowds, no waving branches. Just a few silent women setting out in the gray dawn to perform the last sad rites at the tomb.

The day that changed human history was not a public occasion but a private one. The day when everlasting life broke into earthly time began not with celebration but with tears.

This is still the way Easter breaks into our lives — when we least expect it, when all seems lost. That's when the stone rolls away and the angel speaks and "death is swallowed up in victory" (I Corinthians 15:54).

If it seems too good to be true, this joy that invades our hearts, it seemed so on that first Easter morning, too. Mary Magdalene could not believe what her eyes were telling her; she took Jesus to be a gardener at work early among the graves. Preoccupied with her loss, she barely glanced at the figure standing before her on the path. She had a mournful task to fulfill and —

"Mary."

There in the first light of dawn, Mary stood still. That voice...that tone of loving involvement....

This was the moment, the moment when Jesus called her by name, that

Easter broke like the sunrise into her heart. It is how we recognize Him still. The risen Jesus calls us so personally, comes into our lives so individually, that with Mary Magdalene, we cry out in glad recognition.

And then we do what the women did on that first Easter Sunday. Dropping their spices and ointments, the burdens of their sad errand, they rushed to tell the others.

They set the pattern, these women who were first at the empty tomb — the two-fold pattern of the Christian faith newborn that Easter morning. They met the living Jesus. And they brought the good news to those who grieved.

That's always our role, when it's Easter in our lives: to tell someone else that He is risen.

The Glory of the Easter Story

In the glorious Easter Story
A troubled world can find
Blessed reassurance
And enduring peace of mind . . .
For though we grow discouraged
In this world we're living in,
There is comfort just in knowing
God has triumphed over sin . . .
For our Saviour's Resurrection
Was God's way of telling men
That in Christ we are eternal
And in Him we live again . . .
And to know life is unending
And God's love is unending, too,
Makes our daily tasks and burdens
So much easier to do . . .
For the blessed Easter Story
Of Christ the living Lord,
Makes our earthly sorrow nothing
When compared with this reward.

— *Helen Steiner Rice*

An Easter Carol

Spring bursts today,
For Christ is risen and all the earth's at play.

Flash forth, thou sun,
The rain is over and gone, its work is done.

Winter is past,
Sweet spring is come at last, is come at last.

Bud, fig and vine,
Bud, olive, fat with fruit and oil, and wine.

Break forth this morn
In roses, thou but yesterday a thorn.

Uplift thy head,
O pure white lily through the winter dead.

Beside your dams
Leap and rejoice, you merry-making lambs.

All herds and flocks
Rejoice, all beasts of thickets and of rocks.

Sing, creatures, sing,
Angels and men and birds, and everything....

— *Christina G. Rossetti*

The Hidden Treasure

Arthur Gordon

ONCE, on an ocean liner, I remember there was a sunrise Easter service. I can see it all still: the first spears of light in the east, the wake arrowing away into the dark, the ageless words of the ageless story.

Afterward the other passengers drifted away, and I found myself at the rail with the chief engineer. He was an old Scotsman, practical and blunt, but with a streak of poetry in him. We had become good friends, as sometimes happens on a sea voyage. The horizon was empty; our ship was alone. But the service left me with a strange, exhilarating sense of companionship — of having been part of something unseen but very powerful. When I mentioned this, the old Scot did not seem surprised.

"Aye," he said, "what you felt was the treasure, no doubt." And as the dawn raced over us, he went on to explain what he meant.

It was a bit fanciful, he admitted, and he could not remember where the idea came from — far back in his childhood, perhaps from his old Gaelic nurse — the idea that ever since the first Easter a vast treasure had been accumulating. Not gold, not silver, not anything like that. No, he said, in this invisible treasure-house were stored all the thoughts, all the emotions that Easter had evoked in countless minds and hearts down through the centuries. All the reverence, the awe and wonder, the love and yearning, the gratitude and prayers.

These things, he said, did not just happen and vanish. Like particles of energy, they had their own permanence: none was ever lost. They were all still there — out of sight, certainly; out of time, perhaps — but with an unending reality of their own, a kind of infinite reservoir that could be sensed and drawn upon by human beings.

"And that," he concluded matter-of-factly, knocking out his pipe against the railing, "is what you were feeling just now: the hidden treasure of Easter."

A fanciful thought, indeed, coming from a man who lived and worked with machinery. But after all, is the idea really so farfetched? We're conditioned to think of reality in terms of tangibles, it's true. But deep within us we know that we are not just nerve and sinew, blood and bone, or even the whirling electrons that underlie and sustain such illusions. We are something more. We are hopes and dreams. We are the great paired opposites: joy and pain, anger and tenderness, tears and laughter. Surely, weighed in the ultimate scale, such things count as much as the measurables that surround us.

In any case, I like to think that the old Scotsman was right — that in the legacies of past Easters there is faith to be borrowed, strength to be sought, courage to be found. Each of us has our problems, our areas of weakness, our moments of despair. But still the triumphant cry comes ringing through the ages: Be of good cheer; I have overcome the world.

And it will come again this year, when light pours over the rim of the world and once more it is Easter Day.

The Fragrance of Easter

Sue Monk Kidd

I've decided to celebrate the events of Easter in a unique way this year. I'm going to make a Holy Week bouquet.

The idea came as I read the Scriptures about the last week of Jesus' life. I noticed that many of the events were accompanied by a particular plant. *Why not remember the events by gathering the plants into an arrangement*, I thought. One that would not only decorate my home for Easter, but symbolize the meaning of that special week.

Here are the plants I plan to use in my bouquet:

A palm branch — to represent the events of Palm Sunday.
Grapes and wheat stalks — to symbolize the Last Supper.
A reed of thorns — to depict the mocking of Christ.
A passion flower or poppy (the source of gall) — to represent the Crucifixion.
Aloe, myrrh or other spices — reminders of Jesus' burial.
A white lily — to symbolize the Resurrection.

Whether you choose to create an actual arrangement as I do, or simply reflect on each plant and the event it exemplifies, I believe you and I will create a thing of beauty that will leave the fragrance of Easter in our lives for a long time to come.

No *Alleluia!* for Lent

Marilyn Moore

It all started on Shrove Tuesday night when a group of us gathered together after a "Fat Tuesday Dinner." We were each asked to write the word *Alleluia* on a piece of paper. Next we placed the scraps of paper into a sturdy cardboard box, and then together we went out to the crest of a nearby snow-covered hill. There we buried the box. We were giving up *Alleluia* for Lent — *alleluia* being our conviction that Christ rose from the dead. For forty days we were going to try living without that sense of victory in our lives. *No Alleluia. No Easter. No risen Christ.*

So now, this is Lent for me. Life without the risen Lord. I'm experiencing it as a dark and very difficult time — devoid of grace. I wonder: Can I find forgiveness for yesterday and hope for tomorrow without *Alleluia?* How do I encourage a friend who is ill? And why should I even care about a motherless child, a homeless family, or a hungry nation? Without *Alleluia* my faith is futile.

On Easter morning we're all going to climb the hill, dig up that box and raise our *Alleluias*. Oh, what a glorious moment that will be. Welcome hope! Welcome grace! Welcome happy morning! He is risen! *Alleluia!*

A Spring Verse

Although the calendar says, "Spring,"
And birds sing every minute,
It isn't spring unless your heart
Removes the winter in it.

— *Lydia O. Jackson*

Our Lord has written
the promise of the resurrection,
not in books alone,
but in every leaf in springtime.

— *Martin Luther*

Let him easter in us,
be a dayspring to the dimness of us,
be a crimson-cresseted east.

— *Gerard Manley Hopkins*

heard him use a thousand times to dismiss something as unimportant or trivial.

In 1939, when news reached me that my mother had died unexpectedly in another town, I was alone in my office, numb with grief and loss. There was a Bible on my desk, and I put my hand on it, staring blindly out of the window. As I did so, I felt a pair of hands touch my head, gently, lovingly, unmistakably. The pressure lasted only an instant; then it was gone. An illusion? A hallucination caused by grief? I don't think so. I think my mother was permitted to reach across the gulf of death to touch and reassure me.

And then some years ago, when I was preaching at a Methodist gathering in Georgia, I had the most startling experience of all. At the end of the final session, the presiding bishop asked all the ministers in the audience to come forward, form a choir and sing an old, familiar hymn.

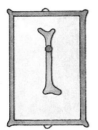was sitting on the speakers' platform, watching them come down the aisles. And suddenly, among them, I saw my father. I saw him as plainly as I ever saw him when he was alive. He seemed about forty, vital and handsome. He was singing with the others. When he smiled at me and put up his hand in an old familiar gesture, for several unforgettable seconds it was as if my father and I were alone in that big auditorium. Then he was gone, but in my heart the certainty of his presence was indisputable. He was there, and I know that some day, somewhere, I'll meet him again.

We don't try to prove immortality so that we can believe in it; we try to prove it because we cannot help believing in it. Instinct whispers to us that death is not the end; reason supports it; psychic phenomena uphold it. Even science, in its own way, now insists that the universe is more spiritual than material. Einstein's great equation indicates that matter and energy are interchangeable. Where does that leave us, if not in an immaterial universe?

The great psychologist William James said, "Apparently there is one great universal mind, and since man enters into this universal mind, he is a fragment of it."

This intangible in all of us, this fragment of the universal mind, is what religion calls the soul, and it is indestructible because — as James said — it is at one with God. The Founder of Christianity said specifically that there is a life beyond the grave. Not only that, Jesus proved it by rising from the dead Himself. If you believe that it happened, death should hold little terror for you. If you don't believe it, you are really not a completely fulfilled Christian.

The Easter message is one of such hope and joy that even unbelievers are thrilled by it. Last year a reporter I know covered the sunrise service that is held each Easter on the rim of the Grand Canyon. It was cold — below freezing, actually — and he had not worn an overcoat. Not a particularly religious man, he stood there shivering dolefully and wishing himself back in bed.

"But then," he told me, "when the sun cleared the canyon rim, and light poured into that stupendous chasm, I forgot all about being cold. One moment everything was gray, formless. Then came torrents of light plunging down the canyon walls, making them blaze with color, dissolving the blackness into purple shadows that eddied like smoke. Standing there, I had a most indescribable feeling, a conviction that the darkness that had filled the great gorge was an illusion, that only the light was real, and that we silent watchers on the canyon rim were somehow a part of the light...."

TRANGE words, coming from a hardboiled reporter, but close to a profound truth. Darkness is powerless before the onslaught of light. And so it is with death. We have allowed ourselves to think of it as a dark door, when actually it is a rainbow bridge spanning the gulf between two worlds. That is the Easter message.

Yet there are people, even good Christians, who accept it with their minds, but really never feel it in their hearts. I know this from personal experience — the message never got through fully to me until I went to the Holy Land and saw with my own eyes the hills and fields and roads where Jesus actually walked.

ONE day we visited the beautiful little village of Bethany. This was the home of Mary and Martha and Lazarus. And there is still a tomb there, said to be the tomb of Lazarus. We went into the tomb, down twenty-two steps and saw the place where the body of Lazarus is presumed to have lain until the voice of Jesus wakened him from the dead. I was so deeply moved that when we came up out of the tomb I turned to my wife and said. "We are standing where the greatest statement ever uttered was made: 'I am the resurrection and the life, he that believeth in Me, though he were dead, yet shall he live' (John 11:25)."

At that moment, for the first time in my life, Easter really happened to me, and I shall never be the same again. For the rest of my days I shall preach, out of a conviction so deep that it can never be shaken, that if people will accept Jesus Christ they will have eternal life.

Years ago I was at Mount Holyoke College in New England, visiting my daughter Elizabeth, a student there. Walking around the campus, we came upon a sundial with an inscription: "To larger sight, the rim of shadow is the line of light."

There you have it in just twelve words. Believe me, death is only a momentary rim of shadow. Beyond it, waiting for all of us who deserve it, is the radiance of eternal life.

The Easter Story

Lord, I rejoice in all the Easter glory
Of Christ triumphant over death and gloom,
Reading again the old, beloved story
Of grieving women — and an empty tomb,
Of men who walked a lonely road in sadness,
Men rendered desolate by loss and fear,
And how their grief was changed to holy gladness;
These are the stories that I love to hear.

Yet, Lord of love, unless I learn to say
With all my heart, "Forgive them, for they know
Not what they do," when others hurt, betray,
Or mock me, and unless I whisper low,
"Thy will be done," when I must suffer pain —
I know I hear the story all in vain.

— Jane Hess Merchant

48

The Little Country Church
Marjorie Holmes

Far from home one Easter morning, our family followed the bells to a little country church.

People hastened to make us welcome, seat us, hand us songbooks already open to the place. The building had the nostalgic smell of most old wooden churches — worn hymnals, pews, carpeting, coffee from countless suppers. Lilies, fragrant on the altar, brought back poignant memories of weddings, funerals and the thrill of childhood Easters.

Familiar, so familiar...the fellowship, the organ, the choir coming down the aisle and the bright fervor of their "Alleluias!" I didn't feel a stranger. Rather, as if I'd come home to something lost.

Then the minister rose, bringing the slight shock of something new: the sideburns, the longish hair, sprouting the non sequitur of a boyish cowlick. For he was so young. ("Still in seminary," somebody whispered.) After this service he'd dash off to another charge. Meanwhile, his enthusiastic presentation of the Easter story: "He isn't there! The tomb is open — the Lord is missing! Or is He? Where has He gone? He has risen! He must be near."

I was really stirred. It was almost like hearing this incredible news for the first time.

At the door I tried to tell him so. "Your sermon was marvelous, very inspiring." Such inadequate words for what I was feeling. Flushing at the compliment, he urged us to come back soon. And as he drove down the hill, past the little church peering down, the cemetery, the grazing cows, the windmill turning — I suddenly realized: "Why, he's younger than Christ was when He began His ministry!"

The old and the new.

A great tenderness filled me — and a hopeful concern. That fiery youth would preach so many Easter sermons in so many places. "Dear Lord," I prayed, "don't let it ever grow old for him. Keep it always new!"

And for me, too.

Easter Symbols of Faith

Van Varner

DOWN through the centuries, long before the first Easter, people have greeted the springtime by taking the commonplace egg and transforming it into a thing of beauty. The egg is the natural symbol of life and fertility, and by dyeing and adorning it, the ancients expressed their joy in the return of the warm sun with its life-giving force. Early on, as these glorified eggs were exchanged among relatives and friends, the primitive designs of sunbursts or wheat or encircling lines symbolized the giver's heartfelt wishes for good health or bountiful harvests or long-lasting life.

And then came Jesus, and His death and resurrection, and as Christianity moved through the world, the decorated egg continued to be a symbol of life — but now with added victorious significance. The old triangular patterns, once standing for the three elements of air, fire and water, now stood for the Trinity of Father, Son and Holy Spirit. The animals representing prosperity — the deer and the horses and rams — remained. But now they were joined by fish, the sign of mutual recognition among early Christians. So it was that pagan and Christian symbols were mixed together, and thus they remain to this day.

In no place in the world has the art of decorating the Easter egg been more beautifully perfected than in the Ukraine. Today, an American family of Ukrainian descent, the Luciows of Minneapolis, have preserved the technique for decorating eggs that was handed down to them from their forebears. The picture displayed here is typical of their handiwork, and it shows the richness and variety of age-old Ukrainian colors and patterns.

Look closely at these lovely Easter eggs. See how many symbols you can find. Do you see the circles that symbolize everlasting life? The geometric combination of crosses and triangles that suggest church steeples? How many different crosses can you find? Notice the design of thorns signifying the crown that Jesus wore, the nets for "fishers of men," the ladders that represent prayers. All of these patterns, and more, make up the beautiful mosaic created by one of humankind's most meaningful and enduring Eastertide customs.

Not What, But Whom

NOT what, but Whom, I do believe,
That, in my darkest hour of need,
Hath comfort that no mortal creed
To mortal man may give; —
Not what, but Whom!
For Christ is more than all the creeds,
And His full life of gentle deeds
Shall all the creeds outlive.

Not what I do believe, but Whom!
Who walks beside me in the gloom?
Who shares the burden wearisome?
Who all the dim way doth illume,
And bids me look beyond the tomb
The larger life to live? —
Not what I do believe,
But Whom!
Not what
But Whom!

— John Oxenham

The Palms

O'ER all the way, green palms and blossoms gay
Are strewn, this day, in festal preparation,
Where Jesus comes, to wipe our tears away
E'en now the throng to welcome Him prepare:

Join all and sing, His name declare,
Let ev'ry voice resound with acclamation,
Hosanna! Praised be the Lord!
Bless Him who cometh to bring salvation!

His word goes forth, and peoples by its might
Once more regain freedom from degradation,
Humanity doth give to each his right,
While those in darkness find restored the light!

Join all and sing, His name declare,
Let ev'ry voice resound with acclamation,
Hosanna! Praised be the Lord!
Bless Him who cometh to bring salvation!

Sing and rejoice, oh, blest Jerusalem,
Of all thy sons sing the emancipation,
Through boundless love the Christ of Bethlehem
Brings faith and hope to thee for evermore.

Join all and sing, His name declare,
Let ev'ry voice resound with acclamation,
Hosanna! Praised be the Lord!
Bless Him who cometh to bring salvation!

– Jean-Baptiste Faure

Little-Egg Words

Lois Millam

A few years ago, when my sons were eight and ten, I found a way to make our children's Easter egg hunt more meaningful.

They would have the usual decorated and candy eggs, I decided — but, in addition, I bought a few dozen inexpensive, pull-apart plastic eggs, the kind that are sold in variety stores in different pretty colors. Then I asked all the members of the family — including the grandmother who'd be visiting Easter Sunday — to choose the one word that best represented Easter to them, and hide it in a plastic egg.

At Easter breakfast we opened the hollow eggs and explained our choice of words. *Glad* was the word young John picked because Easter to him is a time of gladness. Other choices were *faith, sacrifice, forgiveness, love*.

There were surprises, too. John and his older brother Steve had put Bible verses in some of the eggs that hadn't been used. And all of us had sneaked words of love and appreciation for one another into extra eggs.

Now our little eggs with their messages are a family tradition. They have made Easter even more special to us, just as it should be.

A Bad Habit

Pat Sullivan

The Easter I was five, we were in the middle of the Great Depression. There was no money for new dresses for my sisters and me. But Mama dyed some old organdy curtains a lovely shade of mint green. Using a pattern cut from old newspapers, she cut the dresses out. Then she sewed them by hand, making French seams, and added wide ruffled collars. They were the most beautiful dresses I had ever seen.

Easter morning Mama dressed us in our finery, then brushed our hair into long curls and warned us to behave while she got dressed for church. My sisters sat quietly while I fidgeted in a big, scratchy chair. I had a bad habit of chewing on my collars, and soon my beautiful new dress was surely ruined. Ashamed of what I had done, I started to cry. Mama took one look, went to the sewing room and returned with another collar, complete with tiny snaps. She snapped off the chewed-up collar, and snapped on the new one.

"See, honey," she comforted me, "Mama made some extra ones for you — just in case."

I was so relieved to know that she knew my bad habit, anticipated it and forgave me, that I never chewed a collar again.

God knows my sins. He foresaw my shortcomings long before I was born. He still loved me so very much that He sent Jesus to save me and the Holy Spirit to comfort me.

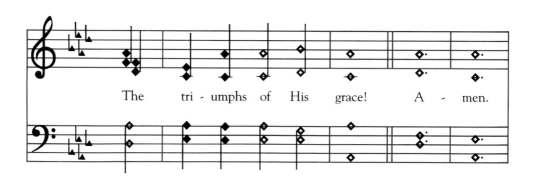

O for a Thousand Tongues

O for a thousand tongues, to sing
My dear Redeemer's praise,
The glories of my God and King,
   The triumphs of His grace!

Jesus! the name that charms our fears,
   That bids our sorrows cease;
'Tis music in the sinner's ears,
   'Tis life, and health, and peace.

Hear Him, ye deaf; His praise, ye dumb,
   Your loosened tongues employ;
Ye blind, behold your Saviour come;
   And leap, ye lame, for joy!

My gracious Master and my God,
   Assist me to proclaim,
To spread through all the earth abroad
   The honours of Thy name.

— Charles Wesley

Faith of a Farmer

A farmer understands deep certainties,
Knows winter is a doorway to the spring,
Walks quiet aisles of prayer where templed trees
Prove resurrection of each living thing.

Steadfast he turns fresh furrows to the sun
And feels new sunlight on his old, old fields;
Each drop of dew and rain an orison
Of hope to guarantee his harvest yields.

He bares his head against an April sky,
Sure of the constant greening of the grass;
When seedlings sprout he does not question why,
Hears trust in wild geese calling as they pass.

A farmer's faith affirms an Easter name
When spring returns a green and living flame.

— Helen Virden

Easter Prayer

We thank thee, God, for spring. When earth
Turns green and ice-freed streams play
Tinkling tunes. The chill wind blows no more,
So blossoms bud. Between sun-stenciled leaves
The first shy warblers trill.

We thank thee, God, for light and soft warm air;
For daffodils whose golden shine adorns
The tufted grass; for woods where hilltops wear
Blue violets for crowns instead of thorns.

We thank thee, God, for life. Now spring is here...
Revive in us fresh understanding, give
New wisdom for the tasks ahead, melt fear
With love...You gave Your Son that we might live.

Dear God, as spring and life return again,
Accept the thanks of grateful hearts. Amen.

— *Ruth W. Stevens*

Our Christ

I know not how that Bethlehem's Babe
    Could in the God-head be;
I only know the Manger Child
    Has brought God's life to me.

I know not how that Calvary's cross
    A world from sin could free:
I only know its matchless love
    Has brought God's love to me.

I know not how that Joseph's tomb
    Could solve death's mystery:
I only know a living Christ,
    Our immortality.

— Harry Webb Farrington

Through the Eyes of Mary

Marilyn Morgan Helleberg

I've been wondering, Mary, about this day we call Palm Sunday. Were you there when they ushered your Son into Jerusalem like a king? Did you watch, proud and silent, from some nearby hill as enthusiasm mounted and garments were spread on the dusty road before Him, palms swaying in acclamation, and shouts of praise resounding in the air? Did you smile and say, "Now isn't that just like Him, to choose a lowly donkey for His mount?" Did you marvel to think that this man (now proclaimed king! Messiah!) once drew sweet nourishment from you?

Did this royal welcome call back for you that other glorious night, when shepherds fell down before your Baby's lowly bed and said they'd heard the angels sing that this, your Son, was born to be a king?

On that day at Jerusalem, while you watched the swaying palms, did you try to remember the feel of His tiny body, asleep in your arms?

I can relate to that. John, my youngest son, is twenty-four now, but I can close my eyes and feel him new and fresh, wrapped in a Winnie-the-Pooh receiving blanket and smelling of Baby Magic. I can't remember the pain of childbirth. The last of it dissolved when Rex kissed my forehead and pronounced those blessed words, all run together, "We-have-a-son-I-love-you." Did Joseph do that, too?

As you watched your Son choose a humble donkey for His steed that day in Jerusalem, did you think back to other times when He'd shown you the glory in common things? I've done that kind of reminiscing, too. One day, during John's sandpile years, he called to me from the porch. "Mommie! Come quick! There's a great big pumpkin in the sky, and cotton candy all around it!" I was in a hurry to finish the dishes. Company was coming. But I'm so glad I dried my hands and went to share the flaming sunset with him. The gift of my senses made fresh with little-boy wonder! What wealth could be a present equal to that?

Ah-h, yes — is that the Palm Sunday message I see through your eyes, Mary? Miracle and majesty abound in common things for those who see with childlike eyes. Truth may be born in a stable, or ride on a lowly donkey, or paint a glory scene across a wide Nebraska sky.

Grandmother Clara's Irish Spring Rite

Elaine St. Johns

Y grandmother Clara, whose maiden name was O'Mahoney, had a rich fund of Irish lore that captivated her grandchildren. Each of us looked forward to her annual weekend rite of spring cleaning. The first time I helped, I found it unsettling — I'd never encountered anyone who had so much to give or throw away.

"But that's perfectly good!" or "You could use that some day!" I would protest. When Grandmother realized I was in real distress she called a story break.

"There was," she said, "this thriving little town in Ireland that the local folk wanted to see grow, so they decided to build a new town hall. But the town fathers decreed, first, that it had to be built on the site of the old town hall. Second, that it had to be built of the same material as the old town hall. Third, that the old town hall had to be kept in use until the new one was completed. And so," she said sadly, "the little town never grew."

"What I'm doing today, Elaine, is not just a work of charity, although that's required of us. I'm making way for the new. New growth starts when you let go of the old."

To this day, because of Grandmother Clara, I do my spring cleaning during Lent. I not only clear away irrelevant material possessions, but I inventory my mental and spiritual household. Then, over the forty days, I try prayerfully to give up the foolish, sterile or limiting thoughts and habits that arrest growth.

"IF any one is in Christ,
he is a new creation;
the old has passed away,
behold, the new has come."

– *II Corinthians 5:17 (RSV)*

Granny's Magical Eggs

Doris Haase

MY family's Easter message that year came unexpectedly. Tindy, our gray-and-white Persian cat, leaped nimbly to the kitchen stool and from there to the refrigerator top. She sniffed at the hard-boiled colored eggs that had been left in a rack to dry. *Crash!* The eggs, intended for the children's Easter baskets, rolled on the floor. I gathered them up, but cracks and lines now spoiled the colorful surfaces.

"They're ruined!" cried Jenny.

Granny thoughtfully studied the situation. Then she sat down, picked up an egg and a wax crayon and began following the crack with a line of green. Soon a vine circled the egg. Then she added tiny green leaves and red, yellow and blue flowers. Like magic, the cracks were transformed. She then went to work on the others and soon all were bright with colorful designs.

"Why, they're prettier than before," Jenny cried.

And they were.

The Easter message? Broken eggs, like broken people, can become more beautiful than ever. The eggs needed Granny. Broken people need Jesus Christ.

A Blooming Tree

Josephine Millard

THE little Arizona town lay parched and lifeless in the heat of the day. The narrow, dusty streets were empty and quiet. At the foot of a sprawling hill of tailing deposited by the copper mill stood the house that was to be our home. In years gone by, it had been painted a dark green, but now it was peeling and dull.

Though I was only nine years old, I was thinking some pretty mournful thoughts as I looked at the drab surroundings, the misshapen tree next door, and I remembered the pleasant home we had left.

In a moment of silence I said in a plaintive voice, "Now we are really poor, aren't we?"

My mother looked at me. Then she said, with an edge in her voice, "Don't ever say we are poor, because we aren't, and we never will be as long as we look for the good things around us. There will be blessings here just as there are everywhere — if we have the eyes to see them. Now please go out and sweep the porch."

I picked up the stubby old broom and went outside. Soon the porch was clean and the sun had dropped suddenly out of sight. And then it happened. A few thin clouds turned pink and lavender in the afterglow, and the hill of waste was bathed in a magical light. The neighbor's huge peach tree seemed to lean across our fence to drop a shower of lovely petals.

The whisper in my soul seemed to repeat the words of my mother: If we search with expectation and faith, we will always find a blooming tree to shower us with petals of hope.

My Rooftop Garden

Margaret Sangster

Y first garden was unlike other gardens, for it grew upon the terrace of a rooftop apartment twenty-two stories above a busy city avenue. Instead of springing from the warm brown earth, it rose gallantly from wooden boxes filled with rich soil by the neighborhood florist. This first garden brought me comfort and peace and eventually a glimpse of glory — for God walked in it.

It came to me when I needed a garden desperately. My heart had been left empty, and my hands without employment. I was resentful and bitter and hurt, for the death of my husband — a young and talented artist — seemed unnecessarily cruel. Why, I kept asking myself, had he been taken away from those who loved him and from the work he loved?

I took up gardening because it was something I had never done before and it carried no ache of a shared memory. And I hoped that the exercise of gardening, even on a small scale, would make me tired enough to sleep at night.

Automatically I dug holes in the dirt and poked seeds in them. While I dug and planted, I was tempted to forget the whole thing, and yet, because I had always tried to finish the projects I started, I plodded on.

But it wasn't until my garden showed life that I became aware of the effort it was making to give me beauty and pleasure. When I saw tender green shoots rising through the ground — when my garden was slightly over a month old — I laughed aloud. The green shoots, feeling their way blindly out of the ground, were like baby kittens whose eyes hadn't opened. They made me feel stronger and lighter, and that's why I laughed. Almost immediately I felt the tears standing in my eyes. They were, in a way, healing tears. For the green shoots had made me aware of one fundamental fact — presence of eternal life, and growth.

The seeds I'd planted were responding to my summons, and there was something in their response that awakened a protective instinct in me. I felt I must shelter the seeds, that I must make it possible for them to justify their existence.

A week later the first heavy rainfall of the season occurred. I had longed for a gentle, refreshing rain — I knew that the little plants needed it — but I hadn't expected a cloudburst. As I stood at my window and watched streams of water beating into the flower boxes, I felt a sick sensation. I was sure that another brave dream was over and done with. I found myself praying inaudibly and inarticulately.

And, miracle of miracles, God answered me — not by making the sky clear and bright, not by making the rain cease to fall — but by drawing my attention to the shoots that had seemed so slender and inadequate. With wondering eyes I noticed that though the rain beat them close to earth, it didn't break them. They bent, but they did not break. Instinctively I knew that when another day dawned and another sun shone, they would be able to lift their faces to the sky.

The first lesson that I learned from my garden was that adversity may bend the spirit, but the spirit need not break. This lesson paved the way for the series of lessons that came, one after another, through the length of the long city summer.

Being a novice at gardening, I wanted to get the best possible results from my flowers in the most personal way. For that reason I planted them all against the inner wall of my rooftop apartment. I had visions of the bower they would make for me and for the guests who, later on, might share my garden with me. I didn't turn my flowers toward the other edge of the terrace — I wanted to possess every inch of them. I wasn't being selfish — not exactly — for I had no neighbors. I lived alone, and lonely, on the top of my own private world.

But as my flowers grew stronger, I discovered they did not agree with my scheme of planting. With an effortless and insistent grace they turned their faces away from me and bloomed — almost every one of them — against the far edge of my wall. They were reaching with unleashed desire toward the sun, which was on the outside. And I realized, with humility, that neither a human hand nor a human agency can turn a growing thing, if it's really a growing thing, away from the light.

Transplanting came next. It taught me that any plant which is stunted in one location may grow amazingly in another. The flowers drooped directly after I had transplanted them, but they didn't droop for long.

IVEN a location that was entirely suited to their needs, they swiftly became joyous and free.

Through these border flowers God told me that life and death are not widely separated one from the other — that dying is just a matter of being transplanted. The distance between earth and heaven, if we have wisdom to understand, is scarcely farther than a space from one flower box to another.

Thinning out — that, too, answered a burning question for me. Some of my blossoms multiplied so rapidly that they filled my boxes to overflowing. When leaves and stems had tangled together in a mass, then faded and finally become brown, I discovered that, to save a proportion of the flowers, I must sacrifice a proportion of them.

And so — without animosity or anger, without a display of favoritism — I uprooted certain plants. I did so hit or miss, not because one plant was better than another, not because I was vindictive or annoyed. And yet, as I dug and pulled and jerked, I found myself wondering whether the discarded plants knew that I was working havoc among them for the greater good of my garden.

The divine plan of God, which at times we resent and fear, seems as apparently ruthless as my method of thinning out a flower box — but it isn't. For though my method was casual, His can never be. The uprooting of one person, instead of another, may be — in His eyes — a gesture toward the ultimate splendor of the universe. We cannot know — not in this life — we can only trust.

And then autumn came to my garden. One by one my plants were touched by the fingers of the frost and folded their hands and went wearily to their well-earned rest. And because by that time my own hands were strong enough to accept work as it came, day by day, and because my heart was no longer empty, and because many of my soul's questions had been answered, I was able to smile at the twisted remnants of fulfillment and to say, "Until another season," rather than, "Farewell forever."

As Long as There Is Hope

HOPE means to keep living
amid desperation
and to keep humming
in the darkness.
Hoping is knowing that there is love,
it is trust in tomorrow
it is falling asleep
and waking again
when the sun rises.
In the midst of a gale at sea,
it is to discover land.
In the eyes of another
it is to see that he understands you.

....

As long as there is still hope
There will also be prayer.

....

And God will be holding you
in his hands.

— *Henri J. M. Nouwen*

Yielding Seed

A lot is asked of a lowly seed
aspiring to be a tree:
Will you give up all that you are
    for what you may someday be,

And fear no more the dark of earth
    — to be buried with the dead —
and with your aim up in the sky,
    dig down in the ground instead?

— *Edward A. Gloeggler*

Chapter
4

The Road to Calvary

"But I, when I am
lifted up from the earth, will draw
all men to myself."

—*John 12:32 (NIV)*

A Broken Star

Sue Monk Kidd

ON Saturday morning I stood on the gloomy porch of the little seaside cottage, gazing at the sky, trying to forget the reasons that had prompted my husband Sandy and me to come to the beach for the Easter weekend. The past months had been fatiguing and painful, with a death in the family and financial setbacks and a number of difficult problems to solve. Hope and perspective had worn thin, and so we'd come here to the cottage overlooking sand dunes and sea oats. As I listened to the waves roar, I wondered if our lives would ever be smooth again.

"How about a walk on the beach," Sandy said. "Maybe you can find a few good shells." Sandy knew well that I'd been a novice collector since I was a child. I loved ocean treasures, and I loved the lure of finding them even more.

I grabbed a bucket; we rolled up our pant legs and headed into a stiff breeze. I walked almost relentlessly down the sandy corridor, as if to walk

away my vague traces of despair. The ocean danced, waves slapping the strand, churning a silver froth. The sun poured a glittering dial of light across the surface that seemed to point us on and on. We hiked a long way, searching the edges of the sea as we went. A few cockles, some periwinkles and a jackknife clam rattled in the bottom of the bucket.

Then, at the rim of a little tidal pool, I spotted a strange silhouette beneath the water. I dipped in my hand and came up with a starfish.

"Look," I cried. "It has only two arms!"

I turned it over; countless white "feet" moved underneath. "It lost three arms and it's still alive," I said with surprise. It gave me a peculiar feeling, like some vaguely remembered dream.

I turned to Sandy. "What do you suppose happened to it?"

"Some predator or maybe a storm," he mused.

My first thought was to throw it back. This was not the sort of specimen you kept for a collection. But something stopped me. Instead, I placed it gently into the bucket, wishing I'd happened on a perfect starfish with five arms, but too attracted to the mutilated little star to put it back. The "star of the sea," as it is sometimes called, had always held a fascination for me. I remembered the old seaman's tale that said starfish were the remains of stars that fell from the sky. I peered into the pail. Broken and wounded, the creature did indeed bring to mind a fallen star.

"Why don't you toss it back?" asked Sandy, noticing my preoccupation.

I shrugged. "I think I'll keep it." It sounded too crazy to mention that I felt a sudden kinship with the star, which had experienced its own loss, too.

Back at the cottage I placed it in a cooler lined with sand and salt water, intended for the crabs we'd failed to net.

Easter Sunday dawned, a pink light streaming in the window. I plugged in the coffee, thinking that we would go home today. Back home to the same circle of problems. Suddenly I felt very tired. I wandered onto the porch and looked in on the starfish. As I stared down into the cooler, looking at the scars where the other three arms had been, I was surprised at the relief I felt that the creature was still alive.

Sandy and I dressed and drove into the little seaside community, searching for a church where we could attend Easter services.

"Let's stop here," I said, as we came upon a small church beside the road. My eyes locked on the sign in front. It said "Star of the Sea Chapel."

We were early. Only a few parishioners had arrived. An usher milled about in the vestibule as we came through the front door.

"Welcome. You folks visiting?" he said.

I nodded. "We're here for the weekend."

There was a natural friendliness to the man. He stood against the door with an easy smile, as though we were neighbors instead of strangers. "Enjoying your stay?"

"It has been very nice," replied Sandy. "Nice and quiet. Mostly we've been walking and picking up shells."

His face lit up, and I suspected he was a collector, too. "It's a good time of year for collecting," he said. ""Finding much?"

"Not much. The best we could do was a starfish missing three arms," I said with a little laugh that sounded more glum than gleeful.

"Of course they grow back," he said offhandedly.

I fell silent. They grow...what did he say?

The usher read my confused look. "The arm of a starfish — it grows back, you know. Some of them can make a brand-new body from a single arm."

"That's amazing," said Sandy.

"They've got an amazing power of regeneration, all right," he said.

The conversation turned to other small talk. More worshipers arrived at the door and our new friend turned to greet them. "Welcome. You folks visiting?" I heard him say to others as we stepped into the sanctuary.

Several times in the Star of the Sea Chapel my mind wandered back to the starfish I'd plucked from the tidal pool. A new starfish from a single arm? The thought of it touched me with awe. What a fine mystery I'd been missing all my life...bits and pieces of starfish growing into new animals.

When we returned to the beach house I took the porch steps two at a time and bent over the cooler. The starfish was there, same as ever. Two arms. Three scars...broken and humble as before. I turned it over and miraculously the tiny white feet moved.

I changed clothes, transferred the star to the bucket, and marched over the dunes, down to the scalloped edge of the sea.

I crouched beside the lacy ruffle of a wave and lifted the star from the bucket. And all at once I remembered it was Easter. Easter! I looked at the broken star as if I were seeing it for the first time. As I held it in my hand the little star spoke to me the message of Easter. It said: When you are broken, wounded, scarred and tired...when you have lost just a little, or so much there is hardly anything left, take heart. That is when God does His most beautiful work.

I felt a new beginning surge in me like the clean sweep of a wave. I knew I could bounce back from my little troubles...from every loss that came my way. For there was new life to be had if I would renew myself in quietness and hope. Like the arm of a starfish.

I laid the broken star on the wet sand. Water tumbled gently over it and when the foam and sizzle cleared away, the star was gone. Vanished, it seemed, into the mystery of Easter.

Ragman

Walter Wangerin, Jr.

saw a strange sight. I stumbled upon a story most strange, like nothing my life, my street sense, my sly tongue had ever prepared me for.

Hush, child. Hush, now, and I will tell it to you.

Even before the dawn one Friday morning I noticed a young man, handsome and strong, walking the alleys of our City. He was pulling an old cart filled with clothes both bright and new, and he was calling in a clear, tenor voice: "Rags!" Ah, the air was foul and the first light filthy to be crossed by such sweet music.

"Rags! New rags for old! I take your tired rags! Rags!"

"Now, this is a wonder," I thought to myself, for the man stood six-feet-four, and his arms were like tree limbs, hard and muscular, and his eyes flashed intelligence. Could he find no better job than this, to be a ragman in the inner city?

I followed him. My curiosity drove me. And I wasn't disappointed.

Soon the Ragman saw a woman sitting on her back porch. She was sobbing into a handkerchief, sighing, and shedding a thousand tears. Her knees and elbows made a sad X. Her shoulders shook. Her heart was breaking.

The Ragman stopped his cart. Quietly, he walked to the woman, stepping round tin cans, dead toys, and Pampers.

"Give me your rag," he said so gently, "and I'll give you another."

He slipped the handkerchief from her eyes. She looked up, and he laid across her palm a linen cloth so clean and new that it shone. She blinked from the gift to the giver.

Then, as he began to pull his cart again, the Ragman did a strange thing: he put her stained handkerchief to his own face; and then he began to weep, to sob as grievously as she had done, his shoulders shaking. Yet she was left without a tear.

"This is a wonder," I breathed to myself, and I followed the sobbing

Ragman like a child who cannot turn away from mystery.

"Rags! Rags! New rags for old!"

In a little while, when the sky showed gray behind the rooftops and I could see the shredded curtains hanging out black windows, the Ragman came upon a girl whose head was wrapped in a bandage, whose eyes were empty. Blood soaked her bandage. A single line of blood ran down her cheek.

OW the tall Ragman looked upon this child with pity, and he drew a lovely yellow bonnet from his cart.

"Give me your rag," he said, tracing his own line on her cheek, "and I'll give you mine."

The child could only gaze at him while he loosened the bandage, removed it, and tied it to his own head. The bonnet he set on hers. And I gasped at what I saw: for with the bandage went the wound! Against his brow it ran a darker, more substantial blood — his own!

"Rags! Rags! I take old rags!" cried the sobbing, bleeding, strong, intelligent Ragman.

The sun hurt both the sky, now, and my eyes; the Ragman seemed more and more to hurry.

"Are you going to work?" he asked a man who leaned against a telephone pole. The man shook his head.

The Ragman pressed him: "Do you have a job?"

"Are you crazy?" sneered the other. He pulled away from the pole, revealing the right sleeve of his jacket — flat, the cuff stuffed into the pocket. He had no arm.

"So," said the Ragman. "Give me your jacket, and I'll give you mine."

Such quiet authority in his voice!

The one-armed man took off his jacket. So did the Ragman — and I trembled at what I saw: for the Ragman's arm stayed in its sleeve, and when the other put it on he had two good arms, thick as tree limbs; but the Ragman had only one.

"Go to work," he said.

After that he found a drunk, lying unconscious beneath an army blanket, an old man, hunched, wizened, and sick. He took that blanket and wrapped it round himself, but for the drunk he left new clothes.

And now I had to run to keep up with the Ragman. Though he was weeping uncontrollably, and bleeding freely at the forehead, pulling his cart with one arm, stumbling from drunkenness, falling again and again, exhausted, old, old, and sick, yet he went with terrible speed. On spider's legs he skittered through the alleys of the City, this mile and the next, until he came to its limits, and then he rushed beyond.

I wept to see the change in this man. I hurt to see his sorrow. And yet I needed to see where he was going in such haste, perhaps to know what drove him so.

The little old Ragman — he came to a landfill. He came to the garbage pits. And then I wanted to help him in what he did, but I hung back, hiding. He climbed a hill. With tormented labor he cleared a little space on that hill. Then he sighed. He lay down. He pillowed his head on a handkerchief and a jacket. He covered his bones with an army blanket. And he died.

O, how I cried to witness that death! I slumped in a junked car and wailed and mourned as one who has no hope — because I had come to love the Ragman. Every other face had faded in the wonder of this man, and I cherished him; but he died. I sobbed myself to sleep.

I did not know — how could I know? — that I slept through Friday night and Saturday and its night, too.

But then, on Sunday morning, I was wakened by a violence.

Light — pure, hard, demanding light — slammed against my sour face, and I blinked, and I looked, and I saw the last and the first wonder of all. There was the Ragman, folding the blanket most carefully, a scar on his forehead, but alive! And, besides that, healthy! There was no sign of sorrow nor of age, and all the rags that he had gathered shone for cleanliness.

Well, then I lowered my head and, trembling for all that I had seen, I myself walked up to the Ragman. I told him my name with shame, for I was a sorry figure next to him. Then I took off all my clothes in that place, and I said to him with dear yearning in my voice: "Dress me."

He dressed me. My Lord, he put new rags on me, and I am a wonder beside him. The Ragman, the Ragman, the Christ!

When I Survey the Wondrous Cross

HEN I survey the wondrous cross
On which the Prince of glory died,
My richest gain I count but loss,
And pour contempt on all my pride.

Forbid it, Lord, that I should boast,
Save in the death of Christ, my God;
All the vain things that charm me most,
I sacrifice them to His blood.

See, from His head, His hands, His feet,
Sorrow and love flow mingled down:
Did e'er such love and sorrow meet,
Or thorns compose so rich a crown?

Were the whole realm of nature mine,
That were a present far too small;
Love so amazing, so divine,
Demands my soul, my life, my all.

— Isaac Watts

My Mother's Easter Bonnet

Joseph Monninger

Y mother was an efficient taskmaster who cooked, cleaned and shopped for nine people on a daily basis. She was a disciplinarian who would make us seven kids walk up and down the stairs a hundred times if we clumped like field hands to dinner. She also enlisted us to help her in the day's chores.

My mother believed that each of her children had a special knack that made him or her invaluable on certain missions. My brother Mike, for example, was believed to have especially keen eyesight. He was hoisted up as a human telescope whenever she needed to see something far away. John was the climber when a kite got caught. My own job was navigator for our gigantic old Chrysler. Only five feet, four inches tall, my mother had difficulty seeing the road ahead. She was not very comfortable gauging distances on the sides either, so as she drove she called for me on the rear seat to yell out clearances. We took corners cautiously, gliding past street signs as a whale glides past an aquarium window.

But my mother's ability to get work done well was only one side of her. She also had an imagination that carried her in different directions, that allowed her to transcend her everyday life. She did not believe in magic as portrayed on a stage, but valued instead the sound of a metal bucket being filled by a hose, or the persistence of a dandelion at the edge of a woodpile.

I recall in particular a small flower box she kept outside the kitchen window in which she raised a crop of basil, oregano, thyme and parsley. In the spring she'd construct a miniature garden, bordered by fences built of chopsticks and paths of dotted dominoes. A pond was made in a seashell; a birdbath was a golf tee. In time the herbs would grow up like a rich forest.

It was here, under the dominoes, that we were instructed to leave our baby teeth. Elves, she told us, would fetch them since birch trees, as anyone knew, could be grown only from a child's first teeth.

I was about six when my mother first touched me with this magic. It was near Easter Sunday, and she had been working flat out to have the house in order for the holiday. There was no reason why she should have paid attention when I came home with an Easter hat I had made in second grade. I was filled with Easter lore, with rabbits and crocuses. And Irving Berlin's "Easter Parade" was playing over and over in my mind.

The hat was made from a paper plate. With spring as the theme, I had cut out flowers, rabbits and suns and pasted them to the bottom of the plate. Thinking it might lend more style to the hat if it wasn't entirely flat, I stapled sprigs of pussy willow to the plate's borders. I cut out a small tree from green construction paper and made a cellophane tape hinge, allowing the tree to bounce up and down and appear suddenly when the wearer descended a step or bent to tie a shoelace.

I don't know what I expected my mother to do with this gift. Perhaps I wanted it to go on the refrigerator door, along with countless other projects I had brought home. I knew that my brothers and sisters, grinning stupidly, would grab it and pretend to put it on, then ask how anyone could think a plate could be an Easter bonnet. As the youngest of our seven, I was hardened to such things.

But my mother's reaction was remarkable. On Easter Sunday, a glorious spring day with blooming forsythia, my mother wore my hat to Mass. She did this in a stately fashion, never showing the slightest embarrassment or discomfort. Stepping out of the car, she pinned my paper plate to her bun, pulled the elastic strap under her chin, and walked slowly toward the church, past men and women dressed up for Easter Sunday. I did not think she would go in; I knew I shouldn't expect her to carry out the entire charade.

She didn't look at me once on this walk; that, I understand now, would have spoiled everything. But I remember watching her float toward the church, the green tree on top of the hat popping up now and then in the wind, the stapled pussy willow twisting and falling over her right ear. I recall feeling a love so wide and full that I could look nowhere but at her as I stepped into the church.

She wore the hat into the pew. Before services began, she slipped it off and placed a more discreet veil over her head. She made no apology. In our imaginary world, the hat was every bit as dignified as the ladies' hats around us. But in the seriousness of the service, reality intervened.

I don't remember what my mother did with the hat after the service. I like to believe the pods of pussy willow went into the flower box to live as hedgehogs, or as boots for elves my mother knew.

By the Way

GO with me, Master, by the way,
    Make every day a walk with Thee;
New glory shall the sunshine gain,
    And all the clouds shall lightened be.
Go with me on life's dusty road
And help me bear the weary load.

Talk with me, Master, by the way;
    The voices of the world recede,
The shadows darken o'er the land,
    How poor am I, how great my need.
Speak to my heart disquieted
Till it shall lose its fear and dread.

Bide with me, Master, all the way,
    Though to my blinded eyes unknown;
So shall I feel a Presence near
    Where I had thought I walked alone.
And when, far spent, the days decline,
Break Thou the bread, dear Guest of mine!

— Annie Johnson Flint

God makes a promise. Faith believes it.
Hope anticipates it. Patience quietly awaits it.

— Author Unknown

LOVE is the fellow
of the resurrection,
scooping up the dust
and chanting, "Live!"

· Emily Dickinson

Christ Knows All

Christ leads me through no darker rooms
than he went through before;
he that unto God's kingdom comes,
must enter by this door...

My knowledge of that life is small,
the eye of faith is dim;
but 'tis enough that Christ knows all,
and I shall be with him.

— *Richard Baxter*

After the Storm

THE storms may come
And limbs may break;
Yet others bend
Beneath the weight —
Of heavy rain
And windy breeze...
A storm can mark
The strongest trees.

Life sometimes deals
With us this way;
In unseen trials
We meet each day.
It's not how much our bodies break
Or how much they may bend;
It's our outlook in our own life
That helps our spirits mend.

— *Hilen Letiro*

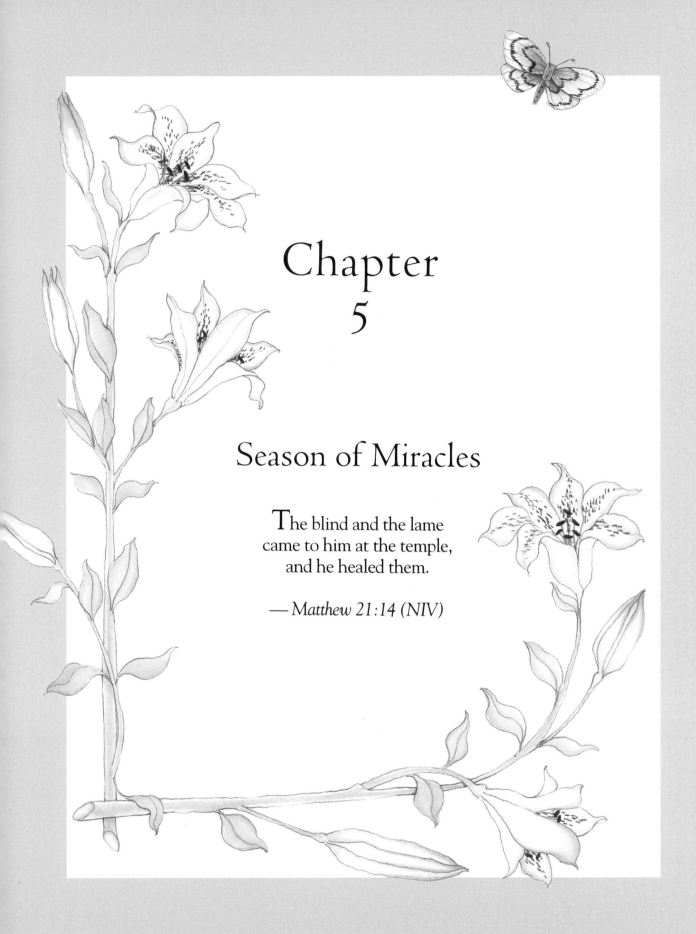

Chapter 5

Season of Miracles

The blind and the lame
came to him at the temple,
and he healed them.

— *Matthew 21:14 (NIV)*

Beatitudes

BLESSED are they of the Easter faith,
For theirs is the risen Lord;
For them He lives, and to them He gives
The fountain of life restored.

Blessed are they of the Easter cheer,
For theirs is the burning heart;
For them the tomb is bereft of gloom,
They walk with their Lord apart.

Blessed are they of the Easter hope,
For theirs is the open gate;
It swings through the tomb to that other room
Where the Lord and our loved ones wait.

— *Clarence M. Burkholder*

Sheep and Lambs

ALL in the April evening,
    April airs were abroad;
The sheep with their little lambs
    Passed me by on the road.

The sheep with their little lambs
    Passed me by on the road;
All in the April evening,
    I thought on the Lamb of God.

The lambs were weary, and crying
    With a weak, human cry.
I thought on the Lamb of God
    Going meekly to die.

Up in the blue, blue mountains
    Dewy pastures are sweet;
Rest for the little bodies,
    Rest for the little feet.

But for the Lamb of God
    Up on the hill-top green,
Only a Cross of shame,
    Two stark crosses between.

All in the April evening,
    April airs were abroad;
I saw the sheep with their lambs,
    And thought of the Lamb of God.

        — *Katharine Tynan*

A mighty fine brown-eyed boy!"

The next day Mrs. McBrodie started sitting with Dixon. The first week, she arrived just after Dixon finished his lunch and watched me rock him to sleep, telling me that her husband was seated near the window across from us with the blind up, so he could signal her if he needed anything.

The second week she started arriving in time to rock the baby herself. The third week she took over his lunch feeding. That's the week I noticed all the blinds pulled up at their house all day.

The fourth week I'd left my typewriter to pace while composing and was suddenly startled to see Mr. McBrodie standing at his window and waving frantically. I thought he was trying to signal his wife, so I ran to the other upstairs window where I could see the nursery downstairs. There, in the nursery window, stood Mrs. McBrodie, holding a laughing, bouncing "Whistle-snapper"! I checked my watch. The baby was awake a half-hour early. I decided I'd better quit for the day and go downstairs, lest Mrs. McBrodie get nervous with him awake.

But when I reached the nursery, the two of them were playing. "I'm glad you're here, though," Mrs. McBrodie said. "Gampy said if the baby woke early to ask if I could take him over to snack with old Gamps." (*Gamps!* I nearly gasped aloud.) She was making funny faces at Dixon, and he was bouncing all over her lap. "That is, if a little fruit, or custard, or homemade cake wouldn't hurt him," she added. When I consented, she held up Dixon's snowsuit to show "Gampy" the verdict, and his joy was as evident as the baby's.

IXON'S "snack time with Gampy" eventually grew to include "playtime with Gampy." And with Dixon soon learning to walk, Gampy came out into the yard on the warmer spring days to watch Gammy walk her chubby charge around the backyard's sidewalks.

Then, the evening before Easter, it happened. My husband and I had left the baby in the usually capable care of our twelve-year-old Dawn, while we shopped for an "Easter surprise" for each child. When we returned an hour and a half later, Dawn came running to meet us in tears. "Mom! Dad! Dixon is locked in the hall closet!" Her words tumbled over themselves. "We were playing tag on hands and knees in the hall.

And I let him get ahead on purpose. I didn't think he'd duck into the open closet and fall against the door! If Gampy and Gammy hadn't been home, I don't know what we'd have done!"

Mr. McBrodie was kneeling on the floor, chisel and hammer in hand, working the pin out of the bottom hinge on the closet door. The top pin, already removed, lay beside his knees. "We almost got you outta there now, Whistle-snapper," Mr. McBrodie was saying, his glasses riding the ridge of his nose as he clanged a blow that sent the pin flying.

My husband and Mr. McBrodie lifted off the door, and Dixon bounced into Gammy's arms delightedly. Suddenly I realized what strenuous work Mr. McBrodie had just done. "You had better sit down," I said. "I hope you didn't overdo!"

"Shucks, I'm not even breathing hard," he answered. "I've got my strength back these days. Been walking every day. I went back to Lodge two weeks ago, and Gammy's wanting me to go to church again. Being that the Whistle-snapper doesn't have any Ohio grandfolks to go to Easter service with, maybe this Gammy and Gampy could kinda stand in for 'em tomorrow if you'd do the driving."

That night, after the excitement, the hugging and the thanking were all over, and the plans were confirmed for tomorrow, I lay in bed thinking it over.

"Why are you chuckling instead of sleeping?" my husband asked.

"I was just thinking," I said. "What a perfect time Easter is for the baby to show me — and the whole neighborhood — that prodding, or maneuvering, or coaxing is not what changes people, but simply God's pure, innocent love shining through us. No wonder the Bible says, 'A little child shall lead them' "(Isaiah 11:6).

"Yes," my husband replied sleepily. "The Whistle-snapper sure brought about a resurrection of another kind this Easter."

"Indeed," I answered as I snuggled deep into my pillow and drifted off to a peaceful sleep. Tomorrow, my heart told me, would be *some kind of Easter*.

A Children's Section

Let the ChildrenCome!

"Do not stop the children....Let them come to me."
— *Mark 10:14 (TBB)*

Butterfly

Waken, sleeping butterfly,
Burst your chrysalis prison.
Spread your beauteous wings and fly,
Christ, the Lord is risen.

— *Joyce Kilmer*

Granny's Ship
Dorothy Dunn

Throughout the Depression years, my brothers, sisters and I often heard our granny say, "One of these days, my ship is coming in." Of course Granny's ship was just a dream — her escape from the reality of being poor most of her life. But to us children it was very real.

Our family got by with the barest of necessities; there rarely was enough left over for special desires. So if we wished for other things, we told Granny about them, and she would plan for them to be aboard her ship.

At times we kids worried greatly as to how the ship was going to arrive at Granny's house in the deep pine woods of East Texas, miles from any waterway. One day when Granny was sitting with us on her front porch, we asked her how she expected her ship to come. Shifting in her rocking chair, she pointed to the marshmallow clouds floating in the bright blue Texas sky.

"Why, children," she explained, "Granny's ship has big beautiful sails. Someday it will rise up on clouds like those, and come floating right up to the front door."

As we grew older, our childish wishes for BB guns, baby dolls and mohair sweaters were replaced by dreams of an education, a job or a lovely wedding. We told Granny of those goals and she put each one aboard her ship.

Granny has been gone a long time now, but I still remember how we sat with her on the porch scanning the skies for her ship. She never told us the name of her ship, but I think perhaps it was Hope. For Granny taught us to have patience, to reach beyond our limitations, and many of our dreams and wishes did indeed come true.

Even now, sometimes, when the skies are brilliantly blue, with soft puffy clouds sailing along with the breeze, I look up — to see Granny's ship. Its sails are full and proud. It is a beautiful ship, carrying a wonderful cargo of many packages of many sizes — all labeled "From Granny, With Love."

Easter Fun!
Easter Egg *"Crayonations"*

Celebrate Easter in a colorful and fun-filled way with kids of all ages. Easter eggs will never be the same with Easter Egg "Crayonations."

Here's what you need:

Crayons • Grater • Old newspapers • Glass jars (for each of your color combinations) • Hot (nearly boiling) water (careful, please!) • Hard-boiled eggs (however many you want to decorate) • Spoon • Egg carton • Clear acrylic spray

Here's what you do:

- Grate crayons over your old newspapers.
- Fill your jar with hot water.
- Drop grated pieces of crayon into water. Use any color combination you want.
- As soon as the crayon begins to melt, put egg in jar and twirl it in the water with your spoon. The melted crayon will make a wonderful design on your egg.
- Carefully remove your egg from the jar and place it in an upside-down egg carton to dry.
- When your egg is dry, use a clear acrylic spray to protect your Easter Egg *Crayonation!*

And remember the most important thing:

HAVE FUN!!

Egg-and-Spoon Race

You may know how to play this.

All those wanting to join in, and it can include grown-ups, line up holding a hard-boiled egg on a spoon. Ready! On your mark! Go! The runners speed off. If an egg is dropped it must be picked up and the runner returns to the starting line to begin again. It can become a long race before someone finally reaches the winning post. Just imagine what it would be like if unboiled eggs were used!

— *Jean Chapman*

Sun Dance

The sun dances
at dawn
On Easter Morn.

For many years people have left their beds to watch the sun rise at the seaside. The first rays, low on the horizon, glint and shimmer in a dance of light.

Here's something to do. Put a large flat container of water in the early morning sun. Or put out a mirror. Watch now! The sun's rays reflected in the water will seem to dance. It is caused by the movement of the air above the water.

— *Jean Chapman*

orning has broken Like the first morning.

Blackbird has spoken   Like the first bird

Praise for the singing!   Praise for the morning!

Praise for them springing   Fresh from the Word.

Morning Has Broken

A carol is a song of joy. Eleanor Farjeon wrote the words of this one for the first day of Spring. The melody is Gaelic and nobody knows who wrote it — the composer is forgotten, but the music is still happily sung.

— Jean Chapman

Morning has broken like the first morning.
Blackbird has spoken like the first bird.
Praise for the singing! Praise for the morning!
Praise for them springing fresh from the word.

Sweet the rain's new fall, sunlit from heaven,
Like the first dewfall on the first grass.
Praise for the sweetness of the wet garden,
Sprung in completeness where His feet pass.

Mine is the sunlight, mine is the morning.
Born of the one light Eden saw play.
Praise with elation, praise every morning,
God's recreation of the new day.

The Fish and the Falls
Max Lucado

The Journey

ONCE upon a distant time, when time was not and rivers had no names, there was a fish.

Born in the cascading bubbles of a rocky mountain stream, this freckled fish learned early the passion of play. He was at home in the water. He raced back and forth in the harbor made by a fallen log. He dared, on occasion, to cross the rapids by darting from rock to rock. Each morning he witnessed the sun lift the shadowy curtain of night. It was his daily invitation to dance in the clean waters. Then, as the sun climbed higher, its warmth would lull him to slowness, giving him time to stare through the waters at the tall trees that waved and the furred visitors whose tongues would drink and then disappear.

But if the day was his time to play, the night was his time to think. This young trout, not content to know so little, kept eyes open while others closed theirs. *What is the source of this stream? Where does it go? Why is it here? Why am I here?* He pondered the questions that others never asked. And he listened at length for the answers.

Then one night he heard the roar.

The night was so bright that the moon saw herself in the stream. The fish, awake with his thoughts, recognized for the first time a noise he'd always heard.

A roar. It rumbled under the river. It vibrated the water. Suddenly the fish knew why the water was always moving.

Who is the maker of this sound? Who is the giver of this noise?

He had to know.

He swam all night without stopping, nourished by his need to know.

The roar grew louder. Its thunder both frightened and compelled him.

He swam until the stars turned pale and the gray pebbles regained their colors. When he could swim no more, weariness overcame curiosity, and he stopped. He slept.

The Encounter

THE sun was warm on the trout's back. In his sleep, he dreamt he was playing again. Dashing between the rocks daring the water to catch him. He dreamt he was at home.

Then he awoke, remembering his pilgrimage.

He heard the roar. It sounded near. He opened his eyes and there it was. A wall of white foam. Water tumbling, then falling, then flying, then crashing.

It was like nothing he'd ever seen.

I will climb it and see it.

He swam to where the water crashed into the river. He attempted to swim upwards. He would ascend the falls by brute force. But the onrush of the water was too strong. Undaunted, he swam until he could swim no more, then he slept.

The next day he attempted to jump to the top. He plunged downward, deep below the churning foam. He swam deep. He swam until the water was still and dark and the roar was distant. Then he turned upward.

His fins fought from one side to the other, pushing and propelling the trout until he was swimming faster than he'd ever swam. He swam straight for the surface. Higher and higher, faster and faster. He raced through the calm waters toward the surface. He broke through the top of the water and soared high into the air. He soared so high he was sure he would land on the top of the waterfall. But he didn't. He barely rose above the foam. Then he fell.

I'll try again. Down he swam. Up he pushed. Out he flew. And down he tumbled.

He tried again. And again. And again. Ever trying to reach the top of the wall. Ever failing at his quest.

Finally night fell and the moon stood vigil over the weary young trout.

He awoke with renewed strength and a new plan. He found a safe pool off to the side of the base of the waterfall. Through the still waters he looked up. He would swim against the gentle trickle of the water as it poured over the rocks. Pleased with his wisdom, he set out. Doggedly he pushed his body to do what it wasn't made to do.

For an entire passing of the sun through the sky he struggled. He pushed on — climbing, falling; climbing, falling; climbing, falling. At one point, when his muscles begged for relief, he actually reached a ledge from which he could look out over the water below. Swollen with his achievement, he leaned too far out and tumbled headfirst into the calm pool from which he began.

WEARIED from his failure, he slept.

He dreamt of the roar. He dreamt of the glory of leaving the mountain stream and dwelling in the waterfall. But when he awoke, he was still at the bottom.

When he awoke the moon was still high. It discouraged him to realize that his dream was not reality. He wondered if it was worth it. He wondered if those who never sought to know were happier.

He considered returning. The current would carry him home.

I've lived with the roar all my life and never heard it. I could simply not hear it again.

But how do you not hear the yearning of your heart? How do you turn away from discovery? How can you be satisfied with existence once you've lived with purpose?

The fish wanted nothing more than to ascend the water. But he was out of choices. He didn't know what to do. He screamed at the waterfall. "Why are you so harsh? Why are you so resistant? Why won't you help me? Don't you see I can't do it on my own? I need you!"

Just then the roar of the water began to subside. The foaming slowed. The fish looked around. The water was growing still!

Then, he felt the current again. He felt the familiar push of the rushing water. Only this time the push was from behind. The water gained momentum, slowly at first, then faster and faster until the fish found himself being carried to the tall stone wall over which had flowed the water. The wall was bare and big.

For a moment he feared that he would be slammed into it. But just as he reached the rocks, a wave formed beneath him. The trout was lifted upwards. Up he went out of the water on the tip of a rising tongue. The wave elevated him up the wall.

By now the forest was silent. The animals stood still as if they witnessed majesty. The wind ceased its stirring. The moon tilted ever so slightly in an effort to not miss the miracle.

All of nature watched as the fish rode the wave of grace. All of nature rejoiced when he reached the top. The stars raced through the blackness. The moon tilted backwards and rocked in sweet satisfaction. Bears danced. Birds hugged. The wind whistled. And the leaves applauded.

The fish was where he had longed to be. He was in the presence of the roar. What he couldn't do, the river had done. He knew immediately he would spend forever relishing the mystery.

Jennie — She Taught Me to Love Spring

Aletha Lindstrom

JENNIE and I met in night school. She had lost her husband, and her daughter was no longer home. My only child, a son, was in college, and my husband had encouraged me to finish work on my degree. After Jennie and I had completed the required courses, we started teaching in the same school. Frequently we had lunch together.

For a time we were just casual friends. But one day, when I was telling Jennie about my problem fourth-grader, we discovered we were kindred spirits. "He's a difficult little character," I explained. "I just can't seem to get through that 'tough-guy' exterior."

Jennie looked thoughtful. "Maybe you're seeing him with your eyes." She was silent a moment and then added softly, "It is only with the heart that one sees rightly."

I stared at her. "You're quoting that! It's from *The Little Prince*, Saint-Exupéry's book for children. One of my favorites. You know it, too?"

Jennie nodded. "I love it. I've read it so often, I've practically memorized it."

Now, when I think of Jennie, I recall that book, because Jennie — more than anyone I know — possessed the gift of seeing with the heart.

From that moment of a treasured book shared, our friendship grew steadily. It wasn't that I didn't have an excellent relationship with my husband and son. But my mother had died shortly after my marriage, and I had neither sisters nor daughters. I realize, now, how I needed someone to share those little, seemingly inconsequential things that add so much to life — things that must be shared to be fully appreciated.

At first it was children's books. I was delighted to find another adult who loved my favorites. Even as I write this, I recall how Jennie and I sat huddled in a coffee shop booth after school, a copy of *Winnie-the-Pooh* open between us. And I smile as I remember the two of us, grown women, laughing until the tears came over the antics of that lovable, silly bear.

One discovery led to another. We found we shared a passion for double-dip strawberry ice-cream cones, for poetry — especially Emily Dickinson and Robert Frost — and for comic strips. Often Jennie would phone me, "Don't miss *Peanuts* tonight!"

And it was Jennie who helped me with my fourth-grade problem child. One day I was at my wit's end with him. "What he needs is a good spanking!" I exploded.

"He's probably had plenty of those," Jennie said. "Maybe he just needs sincere praise for *anything* he does right, and a hug or two each day." I followed this suggestion, and eventually, because of Jennie, I discovered a lovable little boy beneath that "tough-guy" exterior.

And she taught me to love spring. Her joy over grass turning green, tiny buds appearing on trees, and crocuses poking through leftover snow was contagious. One April day I said, "I hate rain!" And I'll never forget what she said. "You can't hate *spring* rain! It brings the flowers!"

So I learned to love spring rain, too, because it did bring flowers — violets, tulips and daffodils. Loveliest of all, I thought, were the pink irises that grew so beautifully in Jennie's garden. "I've never seen such a pretty shade of pink," I told her. "And those ruffled petals — they remind me of a party dress I had when I was little."

That was the day four years ago that she insisted upon getting a spade, digging up one of her two iris roots, and bringing it to my house. We planted it together, but I felt at the time that we hadn't dug deep enough into the earth. Every spring after that Jennie would call and ask, "Is your iris in blossom yet?"

"No," I'd reply. " I told you we didn't plant it deep enough. You'd better come out and look at it."

Then Jennie would drive to our farm from her house in town. After a cup of tea, we'd walk out and inspect the iris.

"Not deep enough?" I'd ask.

Jennie's reply was always the same. "I'm sure it's deep enough. You've just got to have more faith." I admit I didn't have faith. That was Jennie's department. She was long on faith. But still it didn't bloom.

Looking back, I count the many other gifts Jennie gave me. The love of walking, for one thing. We spent hours walking together down country roads and along suburban sidewalks. During those times I discovered the inexpressible comfort of sharing my thoughts and feelings, trusting Jennie would understand — and agree.

HE did, with one exception. Eventually, of course, our discussions turned to God, the Bible and faith. I knew that Jennie was a devout Christian. Still, I had to ask the question, "Do you honestly believe all of God's promises, Jennie? Do you believe *without any doubts?*"

"Yes," Jennie said simply, "without any doubts." I recall that she was quiet for a moment. Then her eyes met mine. "And you?"

I looked away. Of course I believed in God. Some Power must have created the moon, the stars, the earth and everything on it. "Yes," I said, "I believe."

"Without any doubts?"

I felt trapped. How could I burden Jennie with my lack of faith? How could I tell her that I felt dying was extinction, that with it we lost all the simple, lovely things that mean so much — family, friends, books, flowers, even spring rain?

But Jennie was waiting for my answer. And I had to be truthful. "Yes, Jennie," I said at last, "I believe — but with all kinds of doubts." We didn't pursue it. Jennie wasn't the sort to force her beliefs on anyone. And I'd always kept my doubts to myself, perhaps for fear of causing others to lose faith — that faith I longed to share.

Then one morning Jennie died. Suddenly. Tragically. My first reaction was shock. And later, disbelief. Even at the funeral I sat dry-eyed. How could that closed casket hold all that was Jennie — her faith, her understanding, her beautiful, generous spirit, her sense of fun and love of everything good? Jennie who saw with her heart? Jennie who was so full of life and who had so much to give to the world? There had to be some mistake. Or this was a monstrous, obscene joke. I couldn't accept it.

And so I'd answer the phone, hoping to hear Jennie's voice. I'd walk along a street, expecting to see Jennie coming toward me. I'd read a bit of poetry or laugh at a cartoon in a magazine. And I'd think, *I must share this with Jennie.*

One afternoon I drove into town and automatically turned down her street. The garage and house doors were shut and the blinds were drawn — like a closed coffin. Suddenly it struck me full force. Jennie was dead and buried in the dark earth. And all the things that had been Jennie — even the bright moments we'd shared — were dead and buried with her.

A dark shadow moved over my life. The spring days seemed empty and cold. The part of me that had been my friendship for Jennie was an aching void. I resented the first robins; what right did they have to sing since Jennie couldn't hear them? The crocuses and daffodils — they only reminded me that Jennie, who had loved them so much, would never see them again.

But came the night with a soft warm rain. I awakened in the morning and for some reason — I don't know why — I pulled on a robe and stepped outside. The robins were singing and a rainbow painted the sky. And below the rainbow, in my flower border, a pink iris bloomed. After four long years — I could scarcely believe it!

I crossed the rain-wet grass in my bare feet, knelt by the fragile blossom and touched it gently. And I started to cry. A robin came and perched on the fence. He cocked his head and looked at me, comic and puzzled. Suddenly I was laughing and crying at the same time. Then — it was the strangest thing and yet the most natural thing in the world — I knew in my heart that Jennie was beside me, enjoying it all immensely.

And I seemed to hear her ask as plain as if she'd spoken aloud, "Now do you believe?"

This time I answered, "Oh, Jennie, yes, I believe—and without any doubts."

Easter in the Wood

I prayed at Easter in the wood,
And it felt good
To fill my soul with God's great peace,
All cares release.

Kneeling, I felt His presence there
Warm on my hair,
As morning sun came shining through
The beads of dew.
Sunshine and mist and fertile sod
All spoke of God.

While praying I recalled all this —
The traitor's kiss
From one He taught to preach and save,
And He forgave.
Betrayed to men who were not good,
He understood.

I thought of how He'd been denied
When Peter cried
With Scorn, "I do not know this man,"
And then he ran
With tear-blind eyes that scarce could see
Gethsemane.

I prayed at Easter in the wood,
And it felt good
In that great open church of God
Where He has trod.

— *Mary E. Pool*

What the Cross Symbolizes

Martin Luther King, Jr.

EVERY time I look at the cross I am reminded of the greatness of God and the redemptive power of Jesus Christ. I am reminded of the beauty of sacrificial love and the majesty of unswerving devotion to truth. It causes me to say with John Bowring:

> In the cross of Christ I glory,
> Towering o'er the wrecks of time;
> All the light of sacred story
> Gathers round its head sublime.

It would be wonderful were I to look at the cross and sense only such a sublime reaction. But somehow I can never turn my eyes from that cross without also realizing that it symbolizes a strange mixture of greatness and smallness, of good and evil. As I behold that uplifted cross I am reminded not only of the unlimited power of God, but also of the sordid weakness of man. I think not only of the radiance of the divine, but also of the tang of the human. I am reminded not only of Christ at his best, but of man at his worst.

We must see the cross as the magnificent symbol of love conquering hate and of light overcoming darkness. But in the midst of this glowing affirmation, let us never forget that our Lord and Master was nailed to that cross because of human blindness. Those who crucified him knew not what they did.

How Silently?

SILENT night...
> "But the crowds cried out,
> 'Crucify him. Crucify him.'"

Holy night...
> "Then they spat in his face and
> struck him with their fists.
> Others slapped him and said,
> 'Prophesy to us, Christ. Who
> hit you?'"

All is calm...
> "When Pilate saw...that
> an uproar was starting, he took
> water and washed his hands...
> 'I am innocent of this man's blood.'
> All the people answered,
> 'Let his blood be on
> us and on our children.'"

All is bright...
> "And darkness came over the
> whole land until the ninth hour,
> for the sun stopped shining.
> And the curtain of the temple
> was torn in two."

Round yon virgin, mother and child...
    "Who is my mother, and who
    are my brothers?...From now
    on...family divided against
    each other..."

Holy infant...
    "And carrying his own cross, he
    went out to the place of the
    skull."

So tender and mild...
    "And he cried with a loud voice,
    'My God, my God. Why have you
    forsaken me?' "

Sleep...
    "Foxes have holes and birds of
    the air have nests, but the Son
    of man has no place to lay his
    head."

In heavenly peace...
    "Do you think I came to bring
    peace to the earth? I did not
    come to bring peace, but a
    sword."

Sleep in heavenly peace.
    " 'It is finished.' With that,
    he bowed his head and gave up
    his spirit."

"And we beheld his glory, the glory
of the one and only Son."

                              – *Ruth Senter*

Eight Big Drops
Quinn Sherrer

THE other night when I knelt in an old church my eyes focused on the soiled green carpet on the other side of the altar rail. Sometime in the past a minister serving communion had evidently spilled some rich red wine. Eight big drops.

As I glanced up at the empty wooden cross suspended from the ceiling, I felt a quickening in my heart.

"See how much I love you. I shed My blood for you," Jesus seemed to say.

For the first time in my life I really felt Christ's sacrifice. Those eight drops of wine were spilled by accident, I'm sure — but they weren't wasted.

His Hands

The hands of Christ
   Seem very frail
For they were broken
   By a nail.

But only they
   Reach heaven at last
Whom these frail, broken
   Hands hold fast.

— *John Richard Moreland*

Good Friday Prayer

O dear Lord, what can I say to you on this holy night? Is there any word that could come from my mouth, any thought, any sentence? You died for me, you gave all for my sins, you not only became man for me but also suffered the most cruel death for me. Is there any response? I wish that I could find a fitting response, but in contemplating your Holy Passion and Death I can only confess humbly to you that the immensity of your divine love makes any response seem totally inadequate.

Let me just stand and look at you. Your body is broken. Your head wounded, your hands and feet are split open by nails, your side is pierced. Your dead body now rests in the arms of your Mother. It is all over now. It is finished. It is fulfilled. It is accomplished.

Sweet Lord, gracious Lord, generous Lord, forgiving Lord, I adore you, I praise you, I thank you. You have made all things new through your passion and death. Your cross has been planted in this world as the new sign of hope.

Let me always live under your cross, O Lord, and proclaim the hope of your cross unceasingly. Amen.

— *Henri J. M. Nouwen*

A Song at Easter

If this bright lily
　　Can live once more,
And its white promise
　　Be as before,
Why can not the great stone
　　Be moved from His door?

If the green grass
　　Ascend and shake
Year after year,
　　And blossoms break
Again and again
　　For April's sake,

Why can not He,
　　From the dark and mold,
Show us again
　　His manifold
And gleaming glory,
　　A stream of gold?

Faint heart, be sure
　　These things must be.
See the new bud
　　On the old tree!...
If flowers can wake,
　　Oh, why not He?

— Charles Hanson Towne

Chapter 8

Rolling Stones Away

"He has risen...."
— *Matthew 28:7 (NJB)*

I Believe!

The stone wasn't rolled
   away from the tomb
So that Jesus could leave.
   He was already gone.

It was rolled away
   so that doubters like me
Could look in and cry,
   "I believe! I believe!"

— Leroy Thomas

So here's to rolling stones away
to give our Lord the chance He needs
to rise and touch
a troubled, lonely world.
Some call it *Resurrection*.
It's wild with wonder,
It's beautiful and real
Intent on throwing life around
it touches and it heals!

Yes, Easter, you can come
An angel of life I'll be.
I'll roll the stone away
and set you free.

— *Macrina Wiederkehr*

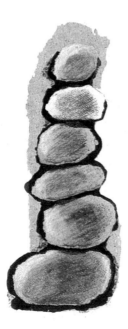

The Sign

William Schmitz

I was on a trip that gray September afternoon when the word came that Frank was dead. Frank, our twenty-year-old son, the baby of our family. I was stunned. I wanted to scream that it couldn't be true.

But it was true. Frank had been killed instantly when the small plane he was flying had gone into a spin and crashed.

All the time during that long trip home, through my tears, I relived in my mind Frank's short life. So much had been crowded into it.

One day when he was thirteen, I found him lying in the street unconscious from multiple injuries from a motor-scooter accident. He spent weeks in the hospital recovering from a skull fracture. During that time Frank had developed a deep personal relationship with God.

As Frank recovered at home, we'd catch him studying the sports pages longingly. He'd been a star baseball and football player in school, but now his damaged body seemed to rule that out. When he was finally able to limp about, he craved exercise and I built a set of outdoor high bars for him.

After the funeral, our two older sons returned to their homes and my wife Polly and I were alone in our grief. I tried to go back to my work as a petroleum geologist but it was useless. I'd sit in my office, turning a pencil over and over in my hand asking, *Why?…why?*

I couldn't seem to do anything any more except think about Frank. "Oh, God," I cried, "please give us some sign…some acknowledgement that he is safe with You."

But Polly and I sank deeper into our depression. One Sunday, however, we took a drive. When we returned home and I reached to turn off the ignition, Polly stiffened and clutched my arm. "Bill, look!" she gasped. She pointed to the earth below the high bars.

I could not believe what I saw. There glowing in the late afternoon sun stood two blood-red lilies in a place where nothing had ever grown before. They grew straight and sturdy from the earth in the same spots Frank had placed his feet to exercise.

Polly and I marveled how they got there. The area had been mowed only a day earlier. We had once placed a swing on the high bar for our grandchildren and the trampled earth was like iron. But there they stood.

The lilies flourished for two weeks. Then they were gone.

But we didn't need them any more to assure us that Frank was safe with Him.

Faith and Doubt

Doubt sees the obstacles,
   Faith sees the way;
Doubt sees the blackest night,
   Faith sees the day;

Doubt dreads to take a step,
   Faith soars on high;
Doubt questions, "Who believes?"
   Faith answers, "I!"

        — Author Unknown

Christ the Lord Is Risen Today

CHRIST the Lord is risen today, Alleluia!
Sons of men and angels say: Alleluia!
Raise your joys and triumphs high, Alleluia!
Sing, ye heavens, and earth reply: Alleluia!

Lives again our glorious King, Alleluia!
Where, O death, is now thy sting? Alleluia!
Dying once, he all doth save, Alleluia!
Where thy victory, O grave? Alleluia!

Love's redeeming work is done, Alleluia!
Fought the fight, the battle won, Alleluia!
Death in vain forbids him rise, Alleluia!
Christ has opened Paradise, Alleluia!

Soar we now where Christ has led, Alleluia!
Following our exalted Head, Alleluia!
Made like him, like him we rise, Alleluia!
Ours the cross, the grave, the skies, Alleluia!

Hail the Lord of earth and heaven! Alleluia!
Praise to thee by both be given, Alleluia!
Thee we greet triumphant now, Alleluia!
Hail, the Resurrection thou! Alleluia!

— *Charles Wesley*

Easter Time

Stark, still
In Friday's sky
The tortured cross beams etch
Their agonizing burden — Christ,
Still...stark.
But wait,
Within three days what miracle!
The stone rolled back; the Christ
Victorious!
Alive!

— Elizabeth Searle Lamb

DEATH has been swallowed up in victory.
Where, O death, is your victory?
Where, O death, is your sting?

- I Corinthians 15:54, 55 (NIV)

153

I Love You, Caleb!

Marion Bond West

"ABSOLUTELY no! Not now, not next year, never," I told Jeremy, one of our thirteen-year-old twins. Since we'd been forced to have our magnificent collie put to sleep after she was hit by a car and badly injured nine months ago, I had refused even to discuss another dog. With God's help I had made it through the pain of Mollie's death, but I was determined never to suffer that way again.

No more dogs for me. I no longer watched the side of the road for strays to rescue, or petted dogs that wandered through our yard. Even though the rest of the family — my husband Jerry, our boys Jon and Jeremy, and our nineteen-year-old daughter Jennifer — desperately wanted another dog, I held out stubbornly. They might be able to love again, but I was not.

Sometimes, though, I found my eyes wandering to the want ads, just "checking" to see if there were "Collies for Sale." For a few seconds I allowed myself to think about having a dog again — but I quickly pushed the idea aside. I would have nothing to do with dogs — ever.

But as hard as I fought it, something was stirring inside me. Almost daily I envisioned a beautiful collie out back — running, jumping, sleeping, even looking in the window at me, its tail wagging. For almost nine months this went on — and it became a joyful habit. When it snowed unexpectedly one day, in my mind a collie pranced in our white backyard. Often when I'd drive into the carport, I'd envision the collie there greeting me. After supper, when there were scraps left over, I mentally gave them to a dog with a long nose and soft brown eyes.

One warm, sunny winter day, my husband went out to the spot where he liked to stretch out on the dry, soft grass. Jerry looked so alone out there without Mollie — she had always followed and sprawled on top of him. In an instant, in my mind, I saw a collie appear — and pounce.

I suppose I missed Mollie most of all early in the morning. That had been our special time together. I'd open the back door just after the sun was up, and she'd be there in a flash, tail wagging. I would sit on the step and she'd put her head in my lap. I'd stroke her long nose and say, "I love you, Mollie Sunshine." Every morning in my mind she was there, waiting to start our day together.

By now I wasn't certain if I was remembering Mollie or imagining a new dog. It didn't seem to matter. The images were comforting, and I could handle a collie who just lived in my mind.

Early one morning, just before time for the school bus, I heard Jon and Jeremy shouting excitedly in front of the house. Holding my robe tightly around me, I hurried out the door and down the steps onto our front lawn. I stopped. There, to my astonishment, stood the collie of my imagination. It could have been Mollie, or Mollie's twin — just standing there wagging its tail!

We all seemed to freeze. The boys didn't move or speak. The dog stood perfectly still, too — even its tail was motionless. I think I might have stopped breathing for a few seconds.

The dog didn't have a collar. The fur underneath its stomach was crusted with mud. He was much too thin and appeared exhausted. But this dog wasn't just an image in my mind, he was *real!*

I dropped to my knees, flung my arms around the collie, and buried my face in its thick fur. Suddenly, something gave way inside of me, and in that instant I knew that the love I'd felt for Mollie wasn't meant to be locked up inside, but meant to flow outward and onward, no matter what happened.

The dog licked my face over and over and put out a paw for shaking. My mind was asking, *Where did you come from? How did you get here?* But my heart was pounding, *Welcome, welcome!*

"Will you feed him, Mama?" Jon asked.

"Of course," I said. "There's the bus, you'd better hurry."

The dog followed me into the backyard almost as though things were familiar to him. He ran around and around in a circle right in Mollie's old tracks. He checked out the doghouse and drank from Mollie's water pan, which we still kept full for the cat.

Can this be? I thought. This dog was doing everything that the dog of my imagination had done. I even had the funny feeling that maybe he'd been somewhere imagining a big yard to play in and a family to adore him.

I fed the hungry visitor almost everything in the house. Finally, he lay down under the oak tree and slept. Back in the kitchen, I stood and watched him. He was there, he was really there.

When our cat, Joshua, ventured out back, the two appeared to be old friends. Joshua and Caleb, I thought to myself, remembering what good friends the biblical *Joshua and Caleb* had been. From then on I called the stray collie "Caleb."

Of course, I knew we had to try to find the owner. But I had this delicious premonition that there wasn't one to find. I called all the vets in the area and waited to see if they had any record of a missing collie. Each time the answer came back over the phone, I breathed a sigh of relief and a prayer of gratitude. I checked with the Humane Society and the pound, leaving my name and number at each location. Then I ran an ad in the paper for a week. The days passed and no one called to claim our Caleb.

I have no reasonable explanation as to where the collie came from or how he got to our house. But somehow I'll always believe that "seeing" a collie daily in our yard for so long, when none was there, had something powerful to do with Caleb's finding us.

Caleb's arrival has taught me that often the very thing you try to avoid the most is the exact thing you need the most. Even though I didn't consciously pray for another collie, I believe God knew the desire of my heart and what I really needed, even before I asked. And if some-day Caleb too is taken from us, I know that God will once again be there to help me through the pain and grief, and prepare the way for new happiness.

Now Caleb and I start each day together. Early in the morning I slip out the back door and Caleb is waiting, just as Mollie used to be. I sit on the steps and he moves as close as he can and puts his head in my lap. We sit there in the sun together, and I rub his long, soft nose and say, "I love you, Caleb!"

What a relief it is to let love flow freely again, and to know with a certainty that — just as it says in Psalm 30:5 — weeping often endures for a night, but joy comes in the morning!

An Easter Song

 song of sunshine
through the rain,
Of Spring across the snow;
A balm to heal the hurts of pain,
A peace surpassing woe.
Lift up your heads, ye sorrowing ones,
And be ye glad at heart,
For Calvary and Easter Day,
Earth's saddest day and gladdest day,
Were just three days apart!

With shudder of despair and loss
The world's deep heart was wrung,
As, lifted high upon His cross,
The Lord of Glory hung —
When rocks were rent, and ghostly forms
Stole forth in street and mart:
But Calvary and Easter Day,
Earth's blackest day and whitest day,
Were just three days apart.

— Susan Coolidge

When a Sparrow Falls

Margaret Cameron

THE day dawned fair and balmy — a perfect Easter Sunday. Long ago, now, but I remember it so well. After a week of chilly rain, the world had burst into bloom. Outside the windows of our bedroom, the dogwood tree spread a canopy of white lace. All down the street, yards were ablaze with azaleas. As I dressed for church, I sang my favorite Easter hymn as blithely as if it had been written just for me:

> *"Welcome, happy morning!"*
> *Age to age shall say....*

I had special reasons to be happy. My husband Ted was minister of his first Episcopal parish in a little town in Virginia. The congregation was small, but growing. As for our family, we were growing, too: In just seven weeks we were expecting our first baby.

Ted had driven ahead of me to church to celebrate early communion. I was to follow on foot in time for the second service at ten. Afterward we would drive to my mother-in-law's home a hundred miles away to join Ted's family for Easter dinner. My doctor had given permission for the trip on the condition I stay overnight and return the next day. I was not to get over-tired!

Dressed in the new maternity suit I had made for the occasion, I started the short walk to church, heavy-bodied but lighthearted. My pregnancy had produced a buoyant sense of vitality. I felt marvelous. Just then the chimes began to ring, and the words of the joyful melody echoed in my mind:

> *Come, ye faithful, raise the strain*
> *of triumphant gladness!*

Members of the congregation were gathering on the church lawn. In those days, ladies still wore hats, and their gay Easter bonnets fluttered like a bouquet. Children scampered out of Sunday school carrying paper baskets of jelly-bean eggs. The senior warden, a snowy-haired gentleman in his eighties, hastened forward to meet me, beaming as always: "Mornin', Miz Parson. The Lord is risen!"

Clasping his hand, I answered with the second half of the traditional centuries-old greeting: "The Lord is risen indeed!"

As the choir lined up to march toward the altar decked with lilies, the congregation poured into the sanctuary ahead of them, filling every pew. Then the organ and voices burst forth, thanking God for the gift of life. Alleluia!

My husband's sermon probably wasn't as brilliant as I proudly thought, but it seemed eloquent to me. Afterward we drove in leisurely fashion through rolling, green countryside to the suburbs of Washington, D.C. As we drove, Easter hymns still reverberated in my ears.

The family dinner was festive — full of fun, banter and compliments. Friends dropped in. Many of them remarked how well I looked. Ted glowed, giving me glances that showed he shared our special oneness, which now united not two persons, but three.

By eleven o'clock we were all in bed at my mother-in-law's house. Surely it had been a blessed Easter!

Suddenly, just before midnight, I woke. No pain, but something was wrong. I was bleeding. Amazed, I shook Ted.

"Wake up, wake up! I think I'm going to have the baby! Tonight!"

My first reaction was excitement, not fear. But his was shock. Sleepy, incredulous, then ghost-pale, he fumbled into his clothes, calling to his mother in the next room.

She put her touseled head in our door, murmuring, "Aren't you just nervous, dear?"

But when she realized I wasn't, she flew to the telephone to ask her doctor for the name of a local obstetrician. Ted bundled me into my bathrobe. As we drove to the hospital, I began to feel very ill.

The young intern's grave expression gave me my first stab of panic. He bent over me, moving his stethoscope from one spot to another on my abdomen, listening, searching.

"You can't find a heartbeat!" I cried.

"It's...unclear," he murmured evasively. "The doctor will be here soon."

And he was, still jauntily attired in green Easter suit and tie. Although we had never met before, I felt at once he was a caring person. He had a warm, confident voice. His hands were gentle as he examined me.

Afterward he conferred with Ted at the door of my room. I heard phrases: "Total placenta separation...baby almost certainly gone."

Anguished, I cried, "Oh, no!" and they approached the bed. I clutched Ted's hand, as another thought struck me.

"I didn't cause this, did I?" I pleaded. "My doctor said I could make the trip."

"No," the doctor reassured me. "We don't know why sudden premature separations occur. But when they do, unless the mother is already in the hospital or a doctor is on hand to operate right away, the baby's supply of oxygen is cut off. When that happens, the baby dies."

Dies! It was hard for me to concentrate on the doctor's next words, but I tried to listen through my tears.

"Unless you lose too much blood, I don't want to operate. If I do, you may have to have operations for deliveries of any other babies you may have. It will be better for you if the baby is born naturally. Do I have your permission not to operate?"

Ted leaned over and held me close, but I couldn't speak.

"Trust me," the doctor urged. "I always try to save the baby if I can without endangering the mother...but in your case — I'm sorry — I have no hope."

What a strong, kind face he had! Perhaps God had sent me such a person in this unfamiliar place. The intern was bringing in an apparatus for a transfusion. I realized that I too could have been in grave danger if I had been in a remote area, far from skilled medical care. I knew I must put myself in the competent hands of this man who had come immediately on a holiday to aid someone he had never heard of before.

I nodded slowly; Ted nodded, too, and we read in each other's eyes, "Good-bye to our Easter baby."

In the long hours that followed, I tried not to give in to despair. We had wanted this baby so much. "Why?" I prayed. "Please tell me why."

How shall I explain the answer that came? I cannot describe it fully; I can only try. While the doctor slept on a cot in the next room and Ted slumped, exhausted, with his forehead on the edge of my bed, a mysterious peace surrounded me. Irresistibly, as if an all-knowing, all-loving Power was gently leading my thoughts, the memory of the morning came back into my mind. I saw the altar, the candles, the lilies. Organ and voices soared again, lifting me beyond sorrow:

He is risen!

He is risen!

Tell it out with joyful voice!

God was telling me something — not an answer to the question, "Why?" He was sending me an even more important message — the message of Easter.

For the first time I understood the meaning of the Resurrection. I saw no vision; I heard no voices, but the message was so clear, so plain:

Because Christ conquered death, your baby lives. Nobody but God may know the unborn child who dies. But He loves and cares for it in the life to come. Like the sparrow that falls, the baby is borne up tenderly in His hands. So don't question. Don't try to understand. Just trust.

The doctor was right; our son never saw the light of day. But he brought to us, his parents, a unique gift. Not just the added strength and closeness that came from shared sorrow. Something even more precious than that.

In the years since that far-away Easter, God has given us three more children; a fine son and two lovely daughters. Each has his or her special gift to offer to us and to life, just as our first son offered his special gift: trust.

Trust, no matter what happens, no matter whether you understand or not, in the wisdom and goodness and love of God.

Opening Our Eyes

CHRIST risen, was rarely recognized by sight.
They had to get beyond the way he looked.
Evidence stronger than his voice and face and footstep
waited to grow in them, to guide their groping
out of despair, their stretching toward belief.

We are as blind as they
until the opening of our deeper eyes
shows us the hands that bless and break
our bread, until we finger
wounds that tell our healing, or witness
a miracle of fish, dawn-caught
after our long night of empty nets. Handling
his word we feel his flesh, his bones, and hear
his voice saying our early-morning name.

— *Luci Shaw*

Chapter
9

Letting Easter In

"Lo, I am with you always,
even to the end of the age."...
— *Matthew 28:20 (NKJV)*

"The Icon Tree"
from The Irrational Season

Madeleine L'Engle

 LESSING is an attitude toward all of life, transcending and moving beyond words. When family and friends gather around the table to break bread together, this is a blessing. When we harden our hearts against anyone, this is a cursing. Sometimes a person, or a group of people, do or say something so terrible that we can neither bless nor curse. They are anathema. We put them outside the city walls, not out of revenge, not out of hate, but because they have gone beyond anything we fragile human beings can cope with. So we say, Here, God, I'm sorry. This is more than I can handle. Please take care of it. Your ways are not our ways. You know what to do. Please.

But sometimes I am confronted with a situation which demands a response of either blessing or cursing, and from me. I cannot refuse to meet the emergency by turning aside. And I have cause to remember Balaam, who was ordered by King Balak to go and curse the children of Israel. Rather reluctantly he saddled his ass and went to do the king's bidding, and his ass stopped in the middle of the road, because she saw something Balaam didn't see; she saw the angel of the Lord standing in the path, and she refused to allow Balaam to go on. And in the end Balaam heeded the ass, and he blessed the children of Israel, blessed instead of cursed.

Blessing is no easier for me than it was for Balaam, and there was a Friday after Easter, two years ago, when I was put to the test.

When we open our house in the country in the spring we know that it will still be winter on our hill; Crosswicks is a good three weeks behind New York, where the Cathedral Close is bursting with blossom, and the cement islands which run down the middle of Broadway are astonishing with the glory of magnolia blooms. At Crosswicks the forsythia will show no bud,

164

though if I bring it indoors it will take only a day or so before it bursts into gold. The house, even with the furnace running, will not be quite warm enough, and we'll huddle around the fire and rush upstairs to bed to plunge beneath the covers. Things which were part of the burden when we lived in Crosswicks year round are fun when it's only on a weekend basis.

I look forward with intense anticipation to the first weekend in the country. Each year the city gets more difficult. Each year the world seems in a worse mess than it was the year before. Our own country is still in trouble, and this trouble is reflected in the city and on the Cathedral Close. I need to get away and find perspective.

On that particular Friday after Easter it had been a bad week in the world, a bad week in the country, a bad week on the Close. I looked forward to the peace and quiet of the first weekend the way, as a small child, I had anticipated Christmas. When we got up to Crosswicks it was still light, one of those rare blue-and-gold afternoons when the sky shimmers with radiance. Hugh said to me, "I bet you're going right to the brook."

"Would you mind?"

"Go ahead, but don't stay too long."

So I called our dog Timothy from sniffing the rock garden and set off across the big field and over the stone wall. Easter was late that year, and the trees were beginning to put forth tiny gold shoots which in another couple of weeks would be green leaves. Some of the budding maples were pale pink, and the beech trees were almost lavender. I could feel myself unwinding from the tensions of the past weeks. I felt surrounded by blessing.

I have several favorite places where I like to sit and think. Probably the most favorite is a large rock above the brook. Directly in front of the rock is an old maple tree. When the trees are fully leafed it is always shaded, and on the hottest day it is cool there. I knew that now the brook would be rushing, filled with clear, icy water from melting snow.

The summer before, I had gone with Josephine and Alan and the two little girls to a fair at Regina Laudis Monastery in Bethlehem, Connecticut. I have a good friend among the Sisters there, and that afternoon she gave me a small, laminated icon of a medieval Mother and Child, and a little cross. I had put these on the trunk of the big maple, and in the late afternoon it was my habit to go to my thinking rock and say my prayers and then, with the icon tree as my focus, to try to move beyond the words of prayer to the prayer of the heart.

So that spring afternoon I headed straight for the rock and the icon tree. But as I started down the tiny path through the trees which lead to the rock, I felt that something was wrong. I quickened my step and when I had climbed up on the rock I saw. Someone had shot the icon at close range. It was split in four parts. There was a bullet hole through the face of the holy child. The cross had been pulled from its ring; only the broken ring still clung to the nail.

I felt an incredible wave of hate flood over me. I was literally nauseated. What had been done had been done deliberately; it was not an accident; it was a purposeful blasphemy, an act of cursing.

I was beyond any response of either blessing or cursing. But I knew that I couldn't go home until I had been washed clean of the hate. The very trees around the rock seemed to draw back in horror and apology because they had not been able to stop the intruder.

Feeling sick and cold I called Timothy and walked and walked.

...

Y dog knew that something had upset me. He kept close as we walked, instead of tearing off in great loops. We kept walking until I had come to the point where I could simply turn over to God whoever had shot the icon and the cross. This person was beyond my puny human ability to understand. I could not add to the curse by cursing. But I did not know how to bless. I went back to the house and told Hugh what had happened. The next day I carried tools and took the remains of the icon off the tree and gave them to the brook. I took away the small nail with the broken loop. Then I sat on the rock and looked at the gouge in the tree's wood. What I describe in the next sonnet did not happen that day, but it did happen, and redeemed the act of hate, and made the tree far more of an icon for me than it was before.

As I sit looking at the shot-at tree
The rough wound opens and grows strange and deep
Within the wood, till suddenly I see
A galaxy aswirl with flame. I do not sleep
And yet I see a trillion stars speed light
In ever-singing dance within the hole
Surrounded by the tree. Each leaf's alight
With flame. And then a burning living coal
Drops hissing in the brook, and all the suns
Burst outward in their joy, and the shot child,
Like the great and flaming tree, runs
With fire and water, and alive and wild
    Gentle and strong, becomes the wounded tree.
    Lord God! The icon's here, alive and free.

BALAK sent Balaam to curse the children of Israel, and the ass saw an angel of God and sat down under Balaam and refused to move, and the curse was turned to a blessing.

I don't understand and I don't need to understand.

Bless the Lord, O my soul, I cry with the psalmist whose songs after all these thousands of years still sing so poignantly for us. O bless his Holy Name, and may he bless each one of us and teach us to bless one another.

Throughout these pages there has been an affirmation, explicit as well as implicit, of my faith in the promise of Easter, of the Resurrection, not only of the Lord Jesus Christ but of us all; the Resurrection not as panacea or placebo for those who cannot cope without medication, or as the soporific of the masses (Simone Weil said that revolution, and not religion, is the soporific of the masses), but as the reality which lights the day.

The experience with the icon tree was a *symbole* of resurrection for me, an affirmation which helps me to respond with a blessing where otherwise I might curse.

There are too many books which affirm resurrection now and can't quite believe in resurrection after death. Resurrection now is indeed important for resurrection then, but resurrection now means little if after death there is nothing but ashes to ashes and dust to dust. The God who redeemed the icon tree for me will not create creatures able to ask questions only to be snuffed out before they can answer them. There is no pragmatic reason why any of my questions should be answered, why this little life should not be all; but the joyful God of love who shouted the galaxies into existence is not going to abandon any iota of his creation. So the icon tree is for me a *symbole* of God's concern, forever and always and unto ages of ages, for all of us, every single one of us, no matter what we think or believe or deny.

So let there be no question: I believe in the resurrection of Jesus of Nazareth as Jesus the Christ, and the resurrection of the body of all creatures great and small, not the literal resurrection of this tired body, this broken self, but the body as it was meant to be, the fragmented self made new; so that at the end of time all Creation will be One. Well: maybe I don't exactly believe it, but I know it, and knowing is what matters.

...

The strange turning of what seemed to be a horrendous No to a glorious Yes is always the message of Easter. The destroyed icon and the wounded tree are a poignant symbol of the risen Christ. The gouge in the tree is beginning to heal, but I will always know that it is there, and it is living witness that love is stronger than hate. Already things have happened which have put this knowledge to the test, and sometimes I have been where I could not go to the rock and see the tangible assurance of the tree's tall strong trunk. But I can turn in my mind's eye and see it, can image the whole chain of events from the cruel destruction of death to the brilliance of new life.

I need to hold on to that bright promise.

There Is No Death

tell you they have not died,
They live and breathe with you;
They walk here at your side,
They tell you things are true.
Why dream of poppied sod
When you can feel their breath,
When Flow'r and soul and God
Know there is no death.

"I tell you they have not died,
Their hands clasp yours and mine;
They are but glorified,
They have become divine.
They live! they know! they see!
They shout with every breath:
All is eternal life!
There is no death!"

— *Gordon Johnstone*

Emmaus

Triumphant!
The victory is secured.
The work is done.
The mission has been accomplished.
Redemption is completed.
What He has come to do
He has done.
He can rejoice.
IT IS FINISHED.

IT IS FINISHED.
He is the victor over sin
And death.

IT IS FINISHED.
He has died — victorious.
He has risen — triumphant.
He can return to the Father.

IT IS FINISHED.

Or is it?

Two walk alone,
Confused, discouraged, tired, defeated.
The long road stretches out before them,
The rumbling city behind,
And on the hill a used cross
And in the garden a sealed tomb.
   He was to be...
   It should have been...
   We thought He was...
   We loved Him.
Triumphant?
What did He come to do?
To die — He did that.
To rise again — Yes, and that.
To love — Ah, yes — to love,

Not just 'til death,
To love and love, forever.

And so, the victorious, triumphant Saviour
Walked again a dusty road,
Fellowshiped with weary travelers,
Broke coarse bread in a humble home,
To teach, to empathize, to love,
Because?
Because He's Jesus.
He came to love
...to show compassion
...to be concerned.

His death didn't change Him,
His resurrection didn't alter Him.
His ascension hasn't affected Him.
He's Jesus.
He's still there to teach,
To heal,
to hold us steady,
To fill our need,
To love.

Our redemption is complete.
IT IS FINISHED.
But Jesus isn't.
He's still at work,
Listening to broken hearts,
Walking dusty roads,
Binding up wounds,
Putting lives back together,
Giving hope and love.

Yesterday ... today ... forever...
That same Jesus.
HE IS NOT FINISHED!
Never!
As long as we need Him.

— *Janette Oke*

Wait Three Days

Patt Barnes

ON that beautiful Easter Monday morning I noticed the old flower lady sitting in her usual place inside a small archway. At her feet corsages and boutonnieres were parading on top of a spread-open newspaper. The flower lady was smiling, her wrinkled old face alive with some inner joy, and on impulse I said to her, "My, you look happy this morning!"

"Why not?" she answered. "Everything is good."

She was dressed so shabbily and seemed so very old that I couldn't help saying, "Don't you have any troubles?"

"You can't reach my age and not have troubles," she replied. "Only it's like Jesus and Good Friday. When Jesus was crucified on Good Friday, that was the worst day for the whole world. When I get troubles I remember that, and then I think of what happened only three days later — Easter and our Lord arising. So when things go wrong, I've learned to wait three days...and somehow everything gets much better."

And she smiled good-bye. But her words still follow me whenever I think I have troubles... "Give God a chance to help...wait three days."

Let Us Go On

SOME of us stay at the cross,
   Some of us wait at the tomb,
Quickened and raised together with Christ,
   Yet lingering still in its gloom;
Some of us bide at the passover feast
   With Pentecost all unknown —
The triumphs of grace in the heavenly place
   That our Lord has made our own.

If the Christ who died had stopped at the cross
   His work had been incomplete,
If the Christ who was buried had stayed in the tomb
   He had only known defeat;
But the Way of the Cross never stops at the Cross,
   And the way of the Tomb leads on
To victorious grace in the heavenly place
   Where the risen Lord has gone.

So, let us go on with our Lord
   To the fulness of God He has brought,
Unsearchable riches of glory and good
   Exceeding our uttermost thought;
Let us grow up into Christ,
   Claiming His life and its powers,
The triumphs of grace in the heavenly place
   That our conquering Lord has made ours.

— Annie Johnson Flint

In Praise of the Resurrection Season

Helen Keller

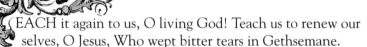

TEACH it again to us, O living God! Teach us to renew our selves, O Jesus, Who wept bitter tears in Gethsemane.

Help us to forget the long way of pain and strife we have come, each of us dragging a cross to some Calvary in our hearts. Help us to forget the hours of utter darkness when we have lost the way. Help us to forget our hates, fears and the bitter thoughts that divide us.

Help us to remember the upclimbing will that is a staff unto our feet. Nourish in us every tiny impulse to help each other. Give us more love, more compassion, more sincerity one to another.

Help us to appreciate the present moment and to search out its advantages that we may be glad for the todays of life, leaving the tomorrows in Thy Hand.

Steady us to do our full stint of work. Help us to rise each day with new sympathies, new thoughts of unity and joy.

Great need have we, this year of all years, to seek the garden where Thou, O Risen Lord, shalt lay on each heart Thy healing Hand.

Give to those who feel downtrodden and neglected the spirit to look up to the sun, to feel its warmth and to appreciate its bright rays. Let them see rainbows in the murky pools, and help them to feel that they are not alone, that Thou from Thy Heavenly Home are watching over them.

Let us be thankful for the resurrection season which revives in us the faith that this circumscribed world in which we live, with its partial visions and unfulfilled dreams, its wearisome struggles and frustrations, is not all there is to life. There is so much to live for!

There is the courageous, useful and unselfish life.

There is much to strive for — to make our cities clean and pleasant,

174

to keep our children healthy, and teach them the honor of work that is worthy of the finest manhood and womanhood, to eradicate from all the fountains of our national life everything that is corrupt. When these commandments of life are kept, there will be resurrection in our souls and in our nation, and our days of tribulation will not have been in vain.

Well may the earth rejoice, lift her head and turn her face to the sun! The sun! The sun that mounts the heavens and makes all things new again!

An Easter Wish

May the glad dawn
   Of Easter morn
   Bring joy to thee.

May the calm eve
   Of Easter leave
   A peace divine with thee.

May Easter night
   On thine heart write,
   O Christ, I live for thee!

— Author Unknown

An Easter Grace

HEAVENLY Creator,
This month we celebrate Easter
and the Resurrection of Your Son.
We rejoice, as we witness the
greening of the world, unfolding in
apple and dogwood blossoms. In
every flower that blooms and every
tree that buds, You have graced us
with the theme of Resurrection:

Christ Lives!

We acknowledge His Presence
at our table, as we offer up this food
to be blessed .
Amen.

— *Terry Helwig*

A Recipe Section

Easter
Blessings
From
Our Table

Jesus said to them, "Come and eat."...
—*John 21:12 (TEV)*

Easter Dinner

Savannah Easter Supper
Charlotte Hale

In my hometown of Savannah, Georgia, Easter for my husband Norris and me is a multi-generational excuse to admire the yard and do nothing special. We need a menu that's simple and that everyone likes, but is festive. Friends, babies, older single people sit on the porch with its old wicker chairs and view of a half-dozen old azaleas covered in pink, dogwood trees wearing white lace veils, the pale yellow Lady Danksia rose and the purple wisteria vines sprawling over the high brick fence and festooning the porch.

Glazed Ham
Dilled Green Beans
Spoonbread

Strawberry Angel Pie
Orange Chiffon Surprise Pie

Glazed Ham

Warm a good pre-cooked ham (any size) according to directions on packaging. (I have the butcher bone, slice and tie ham for perfect presentation.) For the final 30-45 minutes of cooking, coat ham with the following glaze:

Mix 1 cup light brown sugar with 1/2 cup strained apricot preserves, 2 Tbs. lemon juice and 1/4 tsp. cloves. Spread over ham and bake until crust forms. You may decorate with cloves and maraschino cherry halves, if desired.

Optional: Substitute canned crushed pineapple or orange marmalade for apricot preserves.

Dilled Green Beans

You may prepare these earlier in the day, if you like, and quickly reheat before serving.

Cook green beans (I like tips left on) quickly in boiling, *unsalted* water just until tender. Just before serving, mix with Lemon Dill Butter: Melt 1/2 cup unsalted butter; add 2 Tbs. fresh lemon juice and 1 Tbs. dried dill weed.

Use leftover butter on other fresh vegetables or spread it on hot bread, fish or ham.

Spoonbread

4 cups milk	1 tsp. sugar
1 cup cornmeal	4 Tbs. melted butter
2 tsp. salt	6 eggs, separated
1 tsp. baking powder	

Scald milk, add cornmeal and cook until smooth and thick. Add salt, baking powder, sugar and butter. Beat egg yolks and add to cornmeal mixture. Beat egg whites until soft peaks form and fold into batter. Pour into a well-buttered, 3-quart casserole and bake uncovered at 375°F for 25-35 minutes. Serve immediately, and pass the butter!

Note: The meal is ready when the spoonbread is ready, because spoonbread won't wait! Since everything else can be made ahead, however, this dish is well worth the trouble.

Strawberry Angel Pie
6-8 servings

3 egg whites	strawberries, fresh, sliced and sugared
1/4 tsp. cream of tartar	(frozen will do, when fresh
1/4 tsp. salt	berries are unavailable)
3/4 cup sugar	sweetened whipped cream

Lightly butter bottom and sides of a nine-inch pie plate. In large bowl of electric mixer, let egg whites warm to room temperature, about 1 hour. At high speed, beat egg whites with cream of tartar and salt just until very soft peaks form when beater is slowly raised. Gradually beat in sugar, 2 tablespoons at a time, beating well after each addition. Continue beating until very stiff peaks form. Meringue should be shiny and moist. Preheat oven to 275°F. Spread 2/3 of meringue on bottom of prepared pie plate. Use rest to cover side and mound around rim. Bake 1 hour. Cool in pan on wire rack.

To serve: Fill with strawberries, top with whipped cream.

Note: Meringue can be made a week ahead if you keep it in an air-tight tin.

This pie is even more fabulous filled with fresh, ripe peaches!

Orange Chiffon Surprise Pie
1 nine-inch pie

Crust
1 1/2 cups graham cracker crumbs
6 Tbs. melted butter

Reserve 1/2 cup of mixed butter and crumbs. Pat remainder into a deep nine-inch pie pan to form crust. Bake for 15 minutes at 375°F.

Filling

1/4 cup sugar	1/2 tsp. grated orange rind
3 Tbs. flour	2 Tbs. water
3 egg yolks	3 egg whites
2 Tbs. lemon juice	1/8 tsp. salt
3/4 cup orange juice	3 ounces sweet chocolate
(must be well flavored!)	whipped cream

Cook and stir first seven ingredients in a double boiler until thick. Cool. Beat egg whites with salt until stiff. Fold into filling. Grate chocolate into cooled pie shell. Pour in filling and bake at 400°F for 10 minutes. To serve, top with whipped cream and sprinkle with reserved crumbs. Grate on more sweet chocolate to garnish.

Vegetarian Easter Dishes
Vegetarian Croquettes Supper
Phyllis Hobe

A few years ago a California cousin, whom I hadn't seen in years, and his wife were planning to spend Easter Day with us. They are vegetarians and I wondered how I could make them feel comfortable sitting down to a traditional baked ham dinner. Thanks to my local library and natural foods store, I discovered a world of delicious, not to mention healthful, recipes that look every bit as substantial as a roast. One of them is a simple, three-part recipe for soybean croquettes with a mushroom sauce.

Soybean Croquettes

1 1/2 cups soybeans
1 large carrot, grated
1 medium-size onion, chopped
1 stalk celery and leaves, chopped
1/2 tart apple (Granny Smith, if available), chopped
2 Tbs. chopped cilantro
2 Tbs. toasted pumpkin seeds
1 Tbs. wheat germ
1 Tbs. vegetable oil
1/4 tsp. freshly ground pepper
2 egg whites, beaten until stiff but not dry

Soak soybeans in cold water to cover in refrigerator overnight. Next day put soybeans and soaking water in a large pot, bring to a boil, reduce to simmer and cook partially covered for 2 to 3 hours until beans are tender but not mushy. Drain and store in refrigerator until ready to assemble croquettes. Coarsely chop enough soybeans to make 3 cups.

Preheat oven to 350°F.

In a large mixing bowl, combine all ingredients. Form into croquettes. Place on a greased cookie sheet and bake for 25 minutes. Remove from oven and allow to cool for 10 minutes before transferring them to a heated platter. Meanwhile, prepare mushroom sauce.

Mushroom Sauce

1 can vegetarian vegetable soup   1 Tbs. vegetable oil
1 cup mushrooms cut in quarters   1 Tbs. cornstarch

Pour vegetable soup into blender and purée at high speed. Set aside.
Cut up the mushrooms and sauté them in the oil until just cooked but
not browned, tossing the pan frequently. In a measuring cup, mix
cornstarch and 1/2 cup of the soup purée. Add the rest of the soup
purée to the mushrooms in the pan and stir over medium heat. Add
cornstarch mixture and stir with a wire whisk until thickened. Pour
over the croquettes, or serve separately.

Broccoli Casserole
Lorena Pepper Edlen

3 stalks fresh broccoli or 8 ounces frozen broccoli
4 ounces fresh mushrooms, sliced lengthwise
4 spring onions, cut on diagonal into bite-size lengths
1 cup brown rice, cooked until tender
3/4 cup walnut halves broken into two or three large pieces
1 4-oz. can sliced water chestnuts
1 cup Cheddar cheese, shredded
1 cup Monterey Jack cheese, shredded
1 cup sour cream

Trim any tough peel from outside of broccoli stems and cut both stems
and flowerettes into bite-size pieces. Cover with water and cook until
nearly tender. Sauté mushrooms and onions until transparent in either
vegetable oil or water. Put cooked brown rice into three-quart casserole
dish. Top with cooked broccoli, mushrooms and onions, walnuts and
water chestnuts. Cover with cheese and bake at 350°F until cheese is
melted and all the ingredients are hot, about 10 minutes. Serve with
dollops of sour cream on top.

Easter Side Dishes
Texas Easter Favorites
Faye Field

Since spring weather is not definite in Texas, often we have a cold Easter. When the weather was crisp, the family in which I grew up always enjoyed these two recipes.

Crackling Cornbread

2 tsp. butter
1 cup pork cracklings
2 cups cornmeal
2 tsp. baking powder

1 tsp. salt
1 egg
1 cup milk

Preheat oven to 400°F. Put 2 tsp. butter in a 9- or 10-inch pan in oven to heat. In large bowl mix cracklings, cornmeal, baking powder and salt. Then work in the slightly beaten egg. Add milk. Pour batter into heated pan. Cook until brown, about 30 minutes.

Black-Eyed Peas

black-eyed peas (about 1/2 pound)
sausage (amount optional)
1 onion
1 8-oz. can whole tomatoes
1/2 cup water

1 Tbs. sugar
2 1/2 Tbs. chili powder
2 tsp. garlic salt
1/4 tsp. black pepper
2 1/2 tsp. celery salt

Place black-eyed peas in 1 1/2 quarts of boiling water. After the water boils for 5 or 10 minutes, reduce heat and let the peas simmer gently for about an hour and a half.

Brown sausage. Add with other ingredients and continue the simmering for about 30 minutes.

Mint Glazed Carrots
Mary Ruth Howes

My church friends love this dish when I bring it to
our Easter Sunday potluck dinner.

8 large carrots (or 12 small ones)   3 Tbs. butter
1/2 tsp. salt (or to taste)   3/4 tsp. mint leaves (2 sprigs)

Quarter carrots or cut in large julienne strips. Boil in just enough water
to cover for about 10 minutes, or until tender. Drain, reserving liquid for
soup. Add other ingredients, tossing and turning carrots. Stir over low
heat until liquid has thickened and carrots are well coated, about 5-10
minutes. Serve hot. (4-5 servings)

Easter Dinner Treat
Oscar Greene

For Ruby and me, Easter Sunday dinner would be nonexistent without
our son Oscar, Jr. and his wife Marie, who do the cooking. Our forty-
one-mile drive to their home in Londonderry, New Hampshire, is filled
with relaxation, thanksgiving and anticipation. Why? Because we are
treated to this delightful dish.

Pistachio Salad

1 16-oz. can pineapple chunks   1 box pistachio instant pudding mix
1 can mandarin oranges   1 16-oz. container dessert topping

Drain pineapple and mandarin oranges, reserving liquid. Combine
three-fourths of this liquid with pudding mix. Stir mixture until it is
stiff. Add fruit, then three-fourths of dessert topping. Mix well until
mixture is green. Garnish with remaining topping. Chill and serve.

Georgian Pecan Surprises
May Gold Smith

Many of us in Macon, Georgia, had pecan trees in the yard and, as the
pecans ripened, we'd be hoisted up the tree by our dads to shake the

limbs so the nuts would fall faster. Our Easter meal was usually leg of lamb or ham, but we had many favorite traditional side dishes, some of them using these very pecans.

Toasted Pecans

1 pound pecan halves
1/4 cup butter (or margarine)
salt to taste

Preheat oven to 300°F. Place pecans in baking pan large enough to make one layer. Distribute slices of butter on them in random fashion. Place in oven; after 3 minutes, remove pan to stir pecans thoroughly to get them coated with butter. Spread them out again; sprinkle with salt to taste. Taste after 4 minutes to see if done (if not, taste again in 2-minute intervals). Cool. Will keep 1-2 weeks in tin or jar. Can refrigerate, but let pecans get to room temperature or warm them briefly before serving.

Pecan Bites (appetizers)

Stick two halves of pecans together with anchovy paste mixed with cream cheese, or Roquefort cheese mixed with cream cheese, or Cheddar spread.

Asparagus and Mushroom Casserole With Pecans

1 15-oz. can asparagus, drained
1 4-oz. can mushrooms, drained
3 eggs, hard-cooked and sliced
1/4 cup pecans, chopped

1 10 3/4-oz. can cream of mushroom
   soup
3 ounces cheese crackers, crushed
   (low-salt type, if available)

Arrange ingredients in layers in greased casserole, reserving some of the crushed cheese crackers for the top. Bake at 350°F for 30 minutes. Yields 4 to 6 servings.

Vegetable Rice With Pecans

Rice is another traditional item in the deep South.

1 cup rice, raw
2 Tbs. butter
1/2 tsp. salt (optional)
2 cups hot chicken broth
1/2 cup chopped parsley

1/2 cup chopped carrots
1/2 cup green onions, sliced on bias
1/2 cup finely chopped celery
1/2 cup chopped pecans

Sauté rice in butter and salt; pour into a casserole. Stir in broth. Cover and bake 45 minutes at 350°F. Add remaining ingredients and toss lightly. Bake 10 minutes more. Yields 6 servings.

Easter Desserts

Easter Cookies
Patricia Brewster

These Easter Cookies are a family favorite of ours—simple to make as well as delicious. It is a Greek tradition to bake these cookies on Holy Thursday.

2 1/4 cups all-purpose flour
1 1/4 tsp. baking powder
1/4 tsp. salt
1/2 cup butter, softened
1 cup confectioners' sugar
1 egg
2 Tbs. milk
2 tsp. vanilla extract
1 egg yolk beaten with 1 Tbs. milk for glaze
3 Tbs. confectioners' sugar

Preheat oven to 375°F. In a bowl, combine flour, baking powder and salt; set aside. In a separate bowl, beat butter and sugar until light and fluffy. Beat in egg, milk and vanilla. Stir in flour mixture, 1/2 cup at a time, blending after each addition.

Take rounded teaspoons of dough and, using your palms, roll each piece back and forth on a lightly floured work surface until it forms a 6-inch rope. Bring ends together to form a hairpin shape; gently twist "hairpin" 2 or 3 times (see diagram). Lightly pinch ends together. Put on greased baking sheet about 1 inch apart; brush with egg glaze. Bake 10 minutes. Sprinkle with remaining confectioners' sugar. Makes 24.

Easy Easter Basket Cake
Shirley Pope Waite

1 angel cake
1 3 1/2-oz. box instant pudding, lemon or pistachio*
1 8-oz. container dessert topping, or equivalent in whipped cream
green food coloring
1/2 cup coconut
small jellybeans or egg-shaped candies

Break off pieces of cake to mold into the bottom of a rounded bowl. Mix the pudding and pour about 1/3 of it in and around the cake. Fashion two other layers of cake and pudding. (There may be some leftover cake.) Place in refrigerator overnight.

Prior to serving time, pour a few drops of green food coloring into about a teaspoon of water. Place in small bowl and add coconut. Stir to color all of the coconut. Drain coconut on a paper towel to remove moisture.

When ready to serve, invert molded cake onto a serving platter. Frost with topping or whipped cream.

Make a "nest" of the green coconut on top of the cake, and place small egg-shaped candies in the nest.
*You can use any flavor of instant pudding; however, yellow or green seems more appropriate for Easter.

Crackle-Top Molasses Cookies
Flossie Noltemeier

These cookies come out crackled like a gingersnap. They remind me of spring in the Tennessee country, when the baby chicks began cracking out of their shells, just before Easter.

3/4 cup margarine
1 cup sugar
1/2 tsp. salt
2 tsp. soda
1 1/2 tsp. cinnamon

1/2 tsp. cloves
1 cup molasses
2 Tbs. cocoa
4 cups sifted flour

Cream margarine, sugar and salt. Add soda, cinnamon and cloves, mixing well. Stir in molasses and cocoa. Gradually add flour, mixing well after each addition.

Chill dough at least 30 minutes, or until dough is stiff enough to handle. Shape into 1" balls. Place on lightly greased cookie sheet. Bake at 375°F for 10 minutes, or until cookies are browned lightly around the edges. Yield: 6 dozen. Dough may be refrigerated for several days, and baked as needed.

Chocolate Pecan Meringue Cake
May Gold Smith

I learned how to do this fun dessert at age 10, and was often called upon to do it for special occasions. It must be made at least 4 hours ahead, on the afternoon before.

4 eggs, separated
1/2 tsp. cream of tartar
1 cup sugar
1 package devil's food cake mix
1/2 cup pecans, chopped
1 1/3 cups water

1/3 cup vegetable oil
1 1/2 cups whipping cream, chilled
3 Tbs. brown sugar
1 1/2 tsp. vanilla
whole pecans

Heat oven to 350°F. Grease and flour two 9-inch round cake pans. Beat egg whites and cream of tartar in small bowl until foamy (slightly stiff). Beat in sugar, one tablespoon at a time; continue beating until stiff and glossy. Do not underbeat. Rub a bit between fingers to see if sugar still feels grainy; if so, beat a little longer.

Beat cake mix (dry), egg yolks, chopped pecans, water and oil in large bowl on low speed, scraping bowl constantly, until moistened. Beat on medium speed, scraping bowl frequently, for two minutes. Pour batter into pans. Spread half of the meringue over batter in each pan to within 1/4 inch of edge. Bake until meringue is light brown, about 40 minutes (meringue will crack, appear "dry"). Cool 10 minutes. Carefully remove from pans; cool cake completely.

Beat whipping cream, brown sugar and vanilla in chilled small bowl until stiff (with clean, dry blades on mixer!). Fill layers with half of the whipped cream and brown sugar mixture; spread remaining amount over top. Garnish top with whole pecans. Refrigerate at least four hours (longer, if desired).

Polka Dot Cookies
Roberta Donovan

Pastel colors seem to speak of Easter, so perhaps that is why I always enjoy making what we call "Polka Dot Cookies" for my children and grandchildren at that special time of year. The cookies are "dotted" with the pastel M&M candies found in stores at Easter time.

2 cubes (1 cup) margarine, softened	1/2 tsp. salt
1 cup brown sugar	1 tsp. baking soda
2 tsp. vanilla flavoring	1 cup chopped nuts (optional)
2 Tbs. cold water	1 cup pastel M&M candies
2 1/4 cups flour	

Blend margarine and brown sugar. Stir in vanilla and water. Add dry ingredients, along with nuts and M&M candies. Drop by teaspoon on ungreased cookie sheet. Bake 7 or 8 minutes at 350 °F.

These are soft cookies, and it is important to note that cube margarine should be used and not the soft kind.

"An Easter Song" by Susan Coolidge taken from *The Best Loved Religious Poems*. Copyright © 1933 by Fleming H. Revell. Reprinted by permission of Baker Book House.

Abridged version of "The Icon Tree" from *The Irrational Season* by Madeleine L'Engle. Copyright © 1977 by Crosswicks Ltd. Reprinted by permission of HarperCollins Publishers.

"Emmaus" reprinted with permission from Bethel Publishing. Taken from *Quiet Places, Warm Thoughts* by Janette Oke.

"Opening Our Eyes" was originally published as ". . . for they shall see God." Reprinted from *The Secret Trees*, © 1976 by Luci Shaw. Used by permission of Harold Shaw Publishers, Wheaton, IL.

All illustrations are copyright © by the photographers and artists listed below: Thank you to:

Judy Pelikan for the overall book design and the illustrations on the cover, the back cover and pages 1, 2, 3, 8, 9, 11, 22, 23, 50, 51, 60, 66, 67, 71, 76, 77, 78, 81, 88, 94, 95, 96, 97, 108, 114, 115, 119, 130, 131, 136, 142, 143, 153, 157, 162, 163, 175, 177.

Ric Allendorf for the illustrations on pages 37, 62, 63, 69, 121, 132, 170.

James Howland Ballou for the photograph of St. James Church, Salem, MA, on page 192.

Beverly Clausen and Sally Seamans for the music on pages 60, 108.

Joni Gillmore for the illustrations on pages 72-75, 98-101, 124-127.

Pam Levy for the illustrations on pages 38, 39, 41, 42-47, 56, 57, 59, 84-86, 110-113, 146, 147, 164-169, 172.

Holly Meade for the illustrations on pages 102, 103, 104, 149.

Patty O'Leary for the illustrations on pages 58, 107, 155.

Natalia Raphael for the illustrations on pages 82, 83.

Kristin Stashenko for the illustrations on pages 52, 53, 90.

Elivia Savadier for the illustrations on pages 34, 35, 92, 93, 122, 123, 158, 161.

Molly Seamans for the illustration on page 191.

Sally Seamans for the eggs on pages 54, 70, 106.

Permission to reprint the following classic artwork has been granted as follows. Many thanks to:

Scala/Art Resource, NY, for Duccio. La Maesta retro. L'ingresso a Gerusalemme. Siena. Museo dell'Opera Metropolitana K 84644, page 12. Giotto. Bacio di Giuda. Padova. Capella Scrovegni, K 32898, page 16. J. Huguet. La flagellazione di Cristo. Paris. Louvre K 80434, page 18. Giotto. Ingresso a Gerusalemme. Padova. Capella Scrovegni K 36955, page 25. Giotto. Ascensione. Padova. Capella Scrovegni K 26032, page 33. Giotto. Crocifissione. Padova. Capella Scrovegni K 36932, page 64. Cimabue. Crocifisso. Arezzo. S. Domenico, K 49520, page 65.

Bridgeman/Art Resource, NY, DHD 29580 El Greco. Christ Driving the Money Changer from the Temple. London. National Gallery, page 26.

Museo di San Marco, Florence/Superstock, Inc. Women at the Sepulchre of Christ by Fra Angelico. 3815/398590, page 48.

The Vatican Museums & Galleries, Rome/Superstock, Inc. Music Making Angel with Lute by Melozzo da Forli, 900/103750, page 49.

Erich Lessing/Art Resource, NY, 40-13-02/37 Duerer. Hare. Watercolor. Vienna. Graphische Sammlung Albertina, page 190.

The Isabella Stewart Gardner Museum, Boston, MA, for "Retable with Scenes of the Passion," Lorraine, Heins 1981, page 4, "Christ Bearing the Cross," by Giovanni Bellini, page 138, and "Pieta" by Michelangelo, page 141.

Anonymous Master nicknamed Monvaerni, Calvary, Saint James, and Saint Catherine of Alexandria triptych, c. 1484-97, painted enamel on copper, 65.1 cm. h. x 36.4 cm. w., 1931.268. Bequest of Mr. & Mrs. Charles Phelps Taft; The Taft Museum, Cincinnati, OH, page 19.

The Pierpont Morgan Library, NY, for "The Ascension," M.643, p. 32, page 21 and "Christ Washing Feet of Disciples," M.44, f.7, page 116.

"The Healing of the Lame and the Blind," 12th Century Siculo-Byzantine Mosaic from the Cathedral of Monreal, Sicily, page 28.

A Note to the Reader

This original Guideposts book is brought to you by the same editors who prepare *Guideposts*, a monthly magazine filled with true stories of people's adventures in faith.

If you have found inspiration in this book, we think you'll find monthly help and inspiration in the exciting stories that appear in our magazine.

Guideposts is not sold on the newsstand. It's available by subscription only. And subscribing is easy. All you have to do is write:

Guideposts Associates, Inc.
39 Seminary Hill Road
Carmel, New York 10512

For those with special reading needs, *Guideposts* is published in Big Print, Braille and Talking Magazine.

When you subscribe, each month you can count on receiving exciting new evidence of God's presence and His abiding love for His people.